THE 20 BIGGEST MISTAKES
REAL ESTATE SALESPEOPLE MAKE
AND HOW TO CORRECT THEM

Ann Freedman

Prentice-Hall, Inc.
Englewood Cliffs, New Jersey

Prentice-Hall International, Inc., *London*
Prentice-Hall of Australia, Pty. Ltd., *Sydney*
Prentice-Hall of Canada, Ltd., *Toronto*
Prentice-Hall of India Private Ltd., *New Delhi*
Prentice-Hall of Japan, Inc., *Tokyo*
Prentice-Hall of Southeast Asia Pte., Ltd., *Singapore*
Whitehall Books, Ltd., *Wellington, New Zealand*

©1980, by

Prentice-Hall, Inc.

Englewood Cliffs, N.J.

Library of Congress Cataloging in Publication Data

Freedman, Ann
    The 20 biggest mistakes real estate salespeople
make and how to correct them.

    Includes bibliographical references and index.
    1.   Real estate business.   I.   Title.
HD1375.F72   333.33'068'8   80-17447
ISBN 0-13-935023-3

Printed in the United States of America

Dedication

To my dear Mother,
who has been so supportive and encouraging
in all my endeavors.

The Practical Value This Book Offers

"What am I doing wrong?" is a question often asked by real estate salespeople. John, sitting at a desk three feet away, with the same type of properties and opportunities as you had, earned $30,000 last year, while you made considerably less. "What's his secret?" you ask. "John's no smarter than me."

When you are truly concerned and determined, you're ready to throw off adversity. In today's complex real estate market, which is both competitive and computerized, buyers and sellers are far more sophisticated than they were ten or even five years ago. You want to be a professional who is capable of selling "on purpose" rather than "by accident."

There can be no room for mistakes. If you are dissatisfied with your present earnings, then you are probably a victim of at least some of the 20 biggest mistakes real estate salespeople make. *Any one of them can undermine a sale and diminish your income.*

Being innovative and alert helps you to step out of the rutted path that has been grooved by others. *By learning the correct techniques and possible mistakes to avoid, you can assess your performance realistically and make the necessary changes to ensure success.*

This book was conceived out of a professional background of long experience in "the art of selling real estate."

Generalities have been avoided. Actual case histories of true situations are used to punctuate the effect of positive selling. All of the case examples are factual.

Chapter 1 shows you how one salesperson, properly prepared, produced a sale the first time out with a buyer, whereas the previous salesman had failed after having shown 30 houses to the same buyer. Chapter 3 includes a demonstration of how asking the right question at the right time culminated in a sale in which the buyer saw the house, signed the offer to purchase on the same day, and was in the house by the very next day. This was in spite of the fact that she had been looking for two months.

In Chapter 4, you'll see how listening and remembering just one fact enabled the buyers to qualify for a mortgage on a $65,000 house. You will discover in Chapter 11 how not losing control paved the way for quick acceptance of a contract on a $105,000 home.

In Chapter 15, you'll find out how one salesman lost a $1200 commission by not following through. In the same chapter, you'll see how just one phone call to a satisfied seller resulted in two hot listings totaling $96,000.

There's a convincing example in Chapter 20 of the importance of keeping abreast of the latest developments in real estate. An experienced salesman testifies that a new method learned at a particular course helped him earn a $50,000 commission on a $500,000 sale.

This book will help you from the initial customer contact through the final closing. It will show you how to identify and avoid or correct costly errors.

If tripling your present income is a reasonable goal, then you should be motivated to discover and correct your mistakes. You'll come away with definite, positive, and constructive ideas on how to be professional and productive. For example, you'll learn, among many other tips:

- How to use tested techniques to overcome the deadly error of talking too much.
- How to avoid wasting time, separating the suspects from the prospects.
- How to really listen and establish good communication with your buyers and sellers.
- How to list more properties by using the magic listing secret.
- How to ask the right question at the right time to close.
- How to become a master at spotting when your customer is ready to buy.
- How to plan in order to get offers and counteroffers accepted quickly.

THE PRACTICAL VALUE THIS BOOK OFFERS

- How to keep abreast of the latest developments in your profession.
- How to assess your performance realistically.

This is a practical reference book that will work for you as a guide toward improving your sales performance.

If the correction of one mistake results in that next sale or listing, you have immediately earned at least 40 times the cost of your investment in this book.

Where have you heard of better odds?

Ann Freedman

Acknowledgments

This book could not have been written without
the patience and understanding of my husband,
the able assistance of my friend, Pauline Singer,
and the help of my daughter, Dr. Carol Freedman,
during the final stages of writing.
To all three, my deepest gratitude.

Contents

1. Failing to Prepare for a Productive Day **21**

How preparation paid off ... Why Tom failed ... The keys to effective planning ... *The Benefits You'll Gain* ... *Techniques You Can Use to Gain These Benefits* ... Preparing for eight real estate selling situations ... Plan for today—a $25,000 idea ... A checklist for preparing the tools of the trade ... Handy checklists ... Tips on preparing the facts and figures ... How preparing a few facts paid off ... Planning to sell a new listing ... Preparation—the key to a $750,000 sale ... The five P's: Proper preparation prevents poor performance ... An important point to learn from a famous attorney ... *Checklist for Planning a Productive Day*

2. Talking Too Much—A Fatal Mistake! **33**

An effective way to refrain from talking too much ... Spectacular sales story ... The most common error in selling ... How a listing was lost ... Why real estate salespeople talk too much ... *The Benefits You'll Gain* ... *Techniques You Can Use to Gain These Benefits* ... Handling incoming telephone calls ... How talking too much introduces objections—a case in point ... Learn to be brief—the folly of telling it all ... Saving the ammunition ... How the sale was clinched ... Learn the powerful pause technique ... The pause that produced surprising results ... Other harmful habits of talking too much ... *Checklist for Overcoming Talking Too Much*

3. Failing to Ask the Right Question at the Right Time . . . 43

How the right question at the right time made an unbelievable sale unbelievably fast ... *The Benefits You'll Gain* ... Selling isn't telling—it's asking ... *Techniques You Can Use to Gain These Benefits* ... Answer a question with a question ... How and when to ask open-ended questions ... Using tie-downs to get your buyer or seller nodding in agreement ... A few more ways to use questions ... Asking for the order ... A good rule to follow ... How I got a "hot" listing ... Ask—ask—ask ... A point to ponder ... *Checklist for Making Good Use of Questions*

4. Not Mastering the Most Important Real Estate Selling Skill—The Art of Listening 53

What does it mean to listen? ... How listening affects you—a case in point ... *The Benefits You'll Gain* ... *Techniques You Can Use to Gain These Benefits* ... How to listen effectively ... Realizing the difference between hearing and listening ... A common tale of woe ... Concentrating ... Showing your clients that you want to listen ... Asking questions to show you are listening ... Listening with your eyes ... Watching for gestures—what they will tell you ... Hearing and heeding buying signals ... How listening and remembering one fact made it possible for a buyer to qualify for a mortgage on a $65,000 home ... Another point to ponder ... *Checklist for Listening Effectively.*

5. Failing to Use Feedback Advantageously 63

The Benefits You'll Gain ... *Techniques You Can Use to Gain These Benefits* ... Overcoming hesitation ... How to turn objections into reasons to buy ... Using the summary technique ... How an indecisive prospect was converted into a willing buyer ... Using feedback to close easier, faster, and more often ... *Checklist for Using Feedback Advantageously*

CONTENTS

6. Not Properly Qualifying Your Real Estate Buyer and Seller **71**

The Benefits You'll Gain ... Techniques You Can Use to Gain These Benefits ... Dispel the myth that "buyers are liars, sellers are too" ... Emotion motivates ... How one salesperson loses sales ... Analyzing the problem first ... How to qualify with a questionnaire ... Handling inquiries ... How to ask qualifying questions with the quickie questionnaire ... How to qualify a buyer's financial ability ... How to learn more about buyer, seller, and property ... Making good use of extra information ... Using information from the sellers ... Learn to walk in the other person's shoes ... How to establish loyalty ... Advance agreement ... *Checklist for Determining a Qualified Buyer and Seller*

7. Failure to Plan an Effective Listing Presentation **89**

Listing is the name of the game, but not many know how to play ... *The Benefits You'll Gain ... Techniques You Can Use to Gain These Benefits* ... Have a planned, not canned, presentation ... Getting to know the property and the homeowner ... Inspecting the property ... Recording the specifics ... Leaving the price until last ... How to handle "We still want to try to sell it ourselves" ... Personalizing the presentation ... *Checklist for Planning an Effective Listing Presentation*

8. Failure to Execute an Effective Listing Presentation ... **99**

The great listing secret ... Understanding the seller's thinking ... *The Benefits You'll Gain ... Techniques You Can Use to Gain These Benefits* ... Sell the service, not statistics ... Perceive the problem ... Promise the solution ... How to prove it ... Ways to tell and show ... Use testimonial letters for powerful influence ... Persuade ... Keeping the door open ... The return visit ... How to ensure your commission ... It had to be a two-week listing ... Points to ponder ... *Checklist for Executing an Effective Listing Presentation*

9. Failure to Effectively Service the Listing............111

How to avoid a seller's most common complaint ... *The Benefits You'll Gain ... Techniques You Can Use to Gain These Benefits* ... How to obtain correct and complete information ... Verifying mortgage information ... Checking legal description ... Procuring the latest tax information ... Receiving information over the telephone ... Listing what is included and what is excluded ... Advertising media ... Merchandising creatively ... Key rules for writing power-pulling ads ... A few helpful hints ... What response are you getting from your ads? ... How to explain marketing procedures to the seller ... The seller's role ... How the seller's interference triggered a buyer's resistance ... Fulfilling your promise to report regularly ... Extending the listing before it expires ... That extra bit of service ... Keeping in touch after the sale ... In a nutshell ... *Checklist for Effectively Servicing the Listing*

10. The Serious Mistake of Overpricing the Property....127

How a high price was paid for an overpriced listing ... *The Benefits You'll Gain...Techniques You Can Use to Gain These Benefits* ... Convincing the seller through comparables ... Property properly priced is half sold ... Giving honest projections of possible pitfalls ... The Perils of Overpricing ... Discussing terms ... When to get a price reduction ... How to get a price adjustment ... Why not start off with a higher price and come down later? ... In the end, you'll win ... *Checklist for Preventing the Overpricing of the Property*

11. Losing Control of the Selling Process..............137

The Benefits You'll Gain ... Techniques You Can Use to Gain These Benefits ... The key to control—planning ahead ... How to set the stage ... Tested tips for controlling real estate selling situations ... How to overcome the "we'll call you" syndrome ... Taking charge at listing interviews ... How an attorney tried to take charge ...

CONTENTS

Maintaining control at the negotiating table ... How a selling agent refused to be intimidated and saved the sale ... How the selling agent lost control and lost a $90,000 sale ... Wrapping it up ... *Checklist for Control of the Selling Process*

12. Failing to Show the Property Effectively 147

The Benefits You'll Gain ... Techniques You Can Use to Gain These Benefits ... Follow the formula—preparation plus matching property to prospect produces peak performances ... The secret of selecting the right houses ... Previewing can be rewarding ... Arranging appointments ... How many houses? ... In what sequence? ... Planning the best route ... Meeting your prospects ... Arriving at the house ... Permitting the joy of discovery ... How to make the most of each showing ... The tip-off clue ... The last step ... How to make open houses count ... Key review points to ponder ... *Checklist for Showing Property Effectively*

13. Failure to Use the Real Estate Salesperson's Most Effective Clincher 161

The Benefits You'll Gain ... Techniques You Can Use to Gain These Benefits ... Guidelines for storytelling ... A story any time ... When all else fails, tell a story ... Bring on the witnesses ... Always a story ... *Checklist for Using the Real Estate Salesperson's Most Effective Clincher*

14. Failure to Get Offers Accepted Quickly. 169

The Benefits You'll Gain ... Techniques You Can Use to Gain These Benefits ... How to call for an appointment ... Preventing leaks ... How to handle phoning the seller ... The sale before the sale ... Upon arrival ... Directing the seating ... How to disclose the contents of the contract ... Controlling your speech muscles ... A word of caution ... When the seller says, "No! This won't do!" ... Let's collaborate ... Asking, "What do you think?"—a good way to find out ... The magic of "What if?" ... $500 apart ...

Presenting counteroffers ... Camp David meeting—a good example ... How to handle "We'd like to think it over" ... The perils of indecision ... Leaving with something specific ... Reporting the counteroffer ... Cooperating with the selling agent ... Two tips ... The final step ... *Checklist for Getting Offers Accepted Quickly*

15. Not Following Through All the Way.................181

The Benefits You'll Gain ... Techniques You Can Use to Gain These Benefits ... Giving up too soon makes it easy for the next salesperson ... How one agent lost a $1200 commission ... Freshening up your sales presentation with "sales reserves" ... How to determine whom to call and when ... Keeping simple records for profitable follow-up ... Steps to take after the sale ... The danger of taking it for granted ... The sequel—making the most of each closing ... How one call resulted in two "hot" listings totaling $96,000 ... Always remember the rewards ... *Checklist for Following Through All the Way*

16. Failure to Attempt Closing Often Enough...........191

The Benefits You'll Gain ... Techniques You Can Use to Gain These Benefits ... Think closing, think success ... How one salesperon's fear of closing changed the newlyweds' plan to buy ... When to close—follow the A B C rule ... Where is the best place to close? ... Four basic steps to creating an atmosphere of acceptance ... Using closing questions to put your prospect in a favorable frame of mind ... Persuading prospects with powerful sales techniques ... How to lock in the sale ... More ways to close sales ... The question, silence, and then the signature ... Having the contract in full view makes it easier to close ... Objections—opportunities to close ... What to say when they say, "I'd like to have my relatives look at it" ... How to handle the stall: "I'd like to consult my attorney first" ... Ask and ye shall receive ... Which closing technique to use when ... *Checklist for Increasing Your Rate of Closing*

17. Failure to Take Maximum Advantage of the Telephone...**205**

The Benefits You'll Gain ... Techniques You Can Use to Gain These Benefits ... Disciplined use of the telephone for best results ... A friendly smile in your voice will get you a warm response ... Controlling conversation to maintain direction of the call ... Using the phone to get appointments, not to sell ... Inquiry about an advertisement ... What to say when they ask for the address ... How to handle calls to attorneys ... Satisfactorily settling problems between the buyer and the seller ... Helpful hints to improve your telephone personality ... Calls are precious—make them pay off ... *Checklist for Making Maximum Use of the Telephone*

18. Not Using Magic Words and Phrases to Motivate Buyers and Sellers **217**

The Benefits You'll Gain ... Techniques You Can Use to Gain These Benefits ... "You"—a three-letter word with powerful impact ... "Why"—another little word with plenty of power ... Using "when," not "if," for positive results ... When the sale falters, try the fantastic F's: Feel, Felt, and Found ... Some short, simple words to involve buyers and sellers ... How to put a hook into your ad ... Paint a picture to inspire action ... Words that quickly attracted a buyer ... Powerful phrases that work wonders in closing ... More phrases to perk up the ears of your buyers and sellers ... How to avoid words that turn off buyers and sellers ... Using magic words to gain power over your clients ... *Checklist for Using Powerful Words and Phrases*

19. Failure to Spot and Heed "Buy" Signals **229**

The Benefits You'll Gain ... Techniques You Can Use to Gain These Benefits ... Noticing "buy" signals ... Comments buyers make which signify interest ... Listening for more "go" signs ... A $45,000 sale in a half-hour ... Signals sellers flash ... Observing the positive signs of

CONTENTS

body language ... Noticing negative signs ... Watch out
for objections—they can be buying signals ... Making the
most of telltale signs ... The bottom line ... *Checklist for
Perceiving "Buy" Signals*

20. **Neglecting to Reach Out for Growth and
    More Profit.** **239**

*The Benefits You'll Gain ... Techniques You Can Use to
Gain These Benefits* ... Making the review a regular ritual
for a better tomorrow ... A realistic approach to assessing your performance ... Checking your pulse rate to see
how fast you are going ... How to change with the
changing times ... A selling secret—maximize your successes, minimize your failures ... Seven ways to overcome
the slump in selling real estate ... How optimism saved
the sale ... How to sharpen your selling skills and grow ...
How a "pro" earned a $50,000 commission with one new
idea ... Widen your horizons with beneficial side effects
... A worthwhile way to insure your future—specialize ...
Facts ... Conclusion ... *Checklist for Evaluating Your
Selling Effectiveness*

Index **253**

1

Failing to

Prepare for a Productive Day

Tom M. was a young, energetic Realtor. His theory was that if you showed your buyers enough properties, you were bound to hit one that they'd like. In one case, he had worked hard and long racking up mileage as he showed some 30 houses to Alice and Dick R.

I entered the scene when Tom fell ill with the flu. Mr. and Mrs. R. were anxious to find their first home and did not want to waste a Sunday, so they asked me to help them.

My license was only two weeks old at the time. I was inexperienced and knew very little about real estate selling, how to use the Multiple Listing books, or the locations of the various listings. Nevertheless, I was determined to be thorough and to find the right house for the R.'s in the shortest possible time.

Tom, on the other hand, was experienced. Yet, he had shown 30 houses and had failed to get an offer. I showed only three houses and produced a contract the first time out. Why had I succeeded? Let me tell you how it happened.

How preparation paid off

In a friendly, casual manner, using a prepared questionnaire, I systematically interviewed Alice and Dick. From this, I learned that they wanted a three bedroom, two bath house with a large, interesting, and informal family room. The price range was $60,000 to $70,000, and they were interested in two particular neighborhoods.

I now had my clues. "Please meet me at the office on Sunday at 2:00," I suggested. "I know what you have in mind and I'm sure we can find a home that will please you."

Before meeting them, I pored over the Multiple Listing book, which was both new and strange to me. Finally, I found ten houses that seemed to meet all of the R.'s requirements. I made appointments to preview all ten. These houses were in areas totally unfamiliar to me, but, with maps in hand, I eventually found them. From the original ten, I chose three that had everything, especially the large, unusual, informal family room.

Now I was confident. I had found houses that would answer my customers' needs and wants. I had also carefully planned the best and most scenic route to take to get to each one.

As I expected, Alice and Dick liked each of the houses I had carefully selected. The third house was their favorite and they eagerly bought it. In short order, the R.'s were the proud owners of their first home.

The preparation involved in this sale consisted of the following:

1. *Using a prepared qualifying questionnaire* to determine the needs and wants of the customers.
2. *Researching* to find the ten houses that could best answer their requirements.
3. *Previewing* the ten houses to:
    a. become familiar with the features of each house.
    b. become familiar with the neighborhoods.
    c. predetermine the most advantageous routes.
    d. choose the three best houses.
4. *Checking* my tools: car, brochures, maps, rate book, scratch pad, pens, and deposit forms.
5. *Planning* to show the three houses with enthusiasm and optimism.

Why Tom failed

Although Tom was a Realtor with years of experience and knowledge, he had made the mistake of neglecting to take time to properly plan his days with the R.'s. Dashing here and there just to show properties proved to be unproductive. Although I was inexperienced, I succeeded in making my first day out with the R.'s productive. This proved to me that the number of years of experience didn't count as much as following the basic, elementary rule of selling real estate, planning and preparing for each step of the sale.

The keys to effective planning

According to Webster's Dictionary, to *prepare* means: 1) "to make ready for a specific purpose," 2) "to make oneself ready," and 3) "to make things ready." For our use in selling real estate, the definition can be applied as follows: To make ready for a *specific purpose* means to make ready for a *specific situation,* as in:

1. Making appointments.
2. Listing interviews.
3. Writing ads and brochures.
4. Answering incoming calls.
5. Showing properties.
6. Presenting offers and counteroffers.
7. Closing sales.
8. Processing sold properties.

THE BENEFITS YOU'LL GAIN

1. You'll feel assured and optimistic.
2. You'll save time—a salesperson's most valuable asset.
    a) You'll be able to develop important situations to the fullest.
    b) You won't be easily sidetracked.
    c) You won't get involved in irrelevant matters.
3. You'll have essential information to use in preventing and overcoming obstacles.
4. You'll speak in a confident, convincing manner, preventing a poor performance.
5. You'll be considered an authority. Buyers, sellers, and other associates will recognize your expertise. They'll seek you out.

6. Clients and customers will have trust and confidence in you. Consequently, they'll be receptive to your instructions to sign the agreement to sell or buy.

7. You'll win more easily and more often at the negotiating table.

8. You'll make more appointments, have more listings and sales, and you'll do it in less time.

9. All of this means that you'll have a more productive day.

TECHNIQUES YOU CAN USE TO GAIN THESE BENEFITS

Preparing for eight real estate selling situations

From making appointments to processing sold properties, each of the eight real estate selling situations constitutes a sale in itself. Each sale acts as a link in the chain leading up to the time when the sale of the property is finalized and you get paid. Therefore, each and every situation is important.

The fundamentals of preparation for these selling situations happen to be quite similar. They consist primarily of planning your day, preparing your tools, gathering the facts and figures pertinent to the people and properties involved, planning your presentation, and preparing yourself mentally. Although these fundamentals of preparation may seem elementary, you will find that they are essential in effectively conducting real estate business today.

Some salespeople who have been out in the field for a long time are very knowledgeable about the mechanics of real estate, but they often fail to make the most of each selling situation. It may be that they have forgotten, neglected, or perhaps never learned the basic techniques of selling.

You'll discover that the more thoroughly you prepare for these selling situations, the better chance you'll have of completing the chain of sales successfully.

Time and confidence in your ability, due to your experiences, may have a way of making you forget the basics that ensure success. You may get so involved with what appears to be the most profitable or exciting duty of the day that you jump from one project to another at your client's slightest whim, rather than follow through on a pre-planned schedule.

There is a story about a lion that chased one type of game until he spotted another that looked better, and began chasing the new game. After several such instances of racing back and forth from one animal to another, all of them had gotten away and the lion was left tired and hungry. Many real estate agents have the same problem and end up with the same results. They fail to concentrate on *one* goal and follow it through to completion.

Plan for today—a $25,000 idea

An excellent solution to this dilemma is the $25,000 idea sometimes referred to as the "Schwab Story." The story revolves around Ivy Lee, an efficiency expert who approached Mr. Charles Schwab, President of Bethlehem Steel Company, with a simple idea. Mr. Schwab was so greatly impressed with this idea that he sent Lee a check for what he thought it was worth—$25,000. This plan was given considerable credit for turning the then unknown Bethlehem Steel Company into the largest independent steel producer in the world.

Many successful salespeople claim that this idea has helped them in their selling careers. Perhaps you will also find it helpful. The essence of the idea was as follows:

1. List the six most important things you have to do tomorrow.
2. Number them in order of their importance.
3. Tomorrow morning, start working on the first item on your list until it is finished.
4. Then tackle item number 2 in the same way, and proceed through the items in order.
5. Continue doing this until quitting time. Don't be concerned if you only finish the first or second items on your list, for you will be working on the most important ones. The others can wait.
6. Do this every working day. It will give you a system for determining which items are most important and the order of their importance.

This simple, but proven effective technique can be as successful for you as it was for Charles Schwab, and it won't cost you $25,000. A simple form, such as "Things to Do Today" on page 26, will encourage you to follow this system, regardless of temptations to deviate from your schedule. If you are not aware of your major objectives every minute of the day, you will be wasting precious time. If you don't complete your most important projects first, you will be losing precious dollars.

THINGS TO DO TODAY

DATE_____   **COMPLETED**

1_____ ☐

2_____ ☐

3_____ ☐

4_____ ☐

5_____ ☐

6_____ ☐

7_____ ☐

8_____ ☐

9_____ ☐

10_____ ☐

11_____ ☐

12_____ ☐

A checklist for preparing the tools of the trade

No successful salesperson would be caught without every item he or she needs to make a sale at any given moment.

An agent, like any professional, must prepare his tools in order to ensure the most productive day. You can't afford to lose a sale or listing just because the tool you needed was back at the office.

While we all realize the importance of having these tools, we have all had the experience of not having something when we needed it.

In order to avoid such an occurrence you can constantly check up on the tools you need to conduct your real estate business. Here's a list of some of the most essential items:

1. Two or more pens—A sale can be lost if a pen goes dry at a crucial moment.
2. Small note pads—These are useful for jotting down information immediately. They make it easy to transfer information or attach a memo to another paper. Writing frees your mind so that you can concentrate on the next matter.
3. Briefcase
4. Appointment book
5. Monthly calendar-at-a-glance, with large blocks
6. Lined sheets, "Things to Do Today"
7. Hammer, screwdriver, signs
8. Keys, lock boxes
9. Tape measure
10. Maps
11. Listing kit—This includes listing agreements, specific data forms for inspecting properties, competitive market analysis forms, and purchase contracts, including VA and FHA.
12. Selling forms—Deposit receipts, real property disclosure warnings, sellers' computation forms, purchasers' computation forms, any other forms authorized by your broker.
13. Calculator
14. Mortgage amortization tables
15. Qualifying questionnaire
16. Switch sheets—These provide information on backup properties to use when answering ad calls. This method eliminates thinking under pressure and aids in getting appointments.
17. Multiple Listing books and/or brochures

Handy checklists

If you're relying on memory, or just winging it, you're probably striking out in many selling situations. For better results, try using some prepared forms or checklists. You'll discover that they can be a great aid in saving sales.

A real estate salesperson preparing to take off for a selling situation can be compared with an airline pilot who, prior to takeoff, reviews a prepared checklist of essential items. Regardless of his years of flying experience, he continues to use a checklist on each and every flight until the day he retires. His copilot calls out each item on the checklist in order. The pilot investigates and responds, "Check." This system is designed to eliminate the human error of overlooking any one item that might be crucial to the smoothness and safety of the flight.

The same care and caution apply to selling real estate. When you check off items on a simple, prepared form, you won't forget or overlook any bit of information that might be crucial to the smoothness and success of your sale. Through constant use, you will become familiar with the checklists that are easy and comfortable for you to use, particularly when you're under pressure. In addition, you'll have written records for your reference file.

Earlier in this chapter I included two handy checklists, one for planning your day and the other for preparing your tools. In later chapters there will be some sample checklists to guide you when you are qualifying a buyer on the telephone or in person, inspecting the property for a listing, presenting comparables of properties to the seller, instructing the seller regarding his role and explaining your role in the procedure of selling his house, and keeping current records on the progress of your sold properties. When you prepare for the various selling situations, you can either use these checklists or adapt them to suit your particular needs, your prospects, and your locality.

Tips on preparing the facts and figures

In any selling situation, inaccurate or incomplete information can be harmful to the sale. To help you avoid making such errors, here are a couple of tips. First, ask probing questions. You'll find that this eliminates much guesswork. Verify, research, and record all of the details, all of the facts and figures. Sometimes you may think it is easier and safe to accept whatever an owner tells you or to copy from a previous brochure, but that isn't so. Protect yourself by using only official sources to provide you with complete and accurate information.

How preparing a few facts paid off

Recently, I ran into Phoebe, an experienced broker who was on her way to present a low offer on an expired listing. She was quite concerned and asked if I would like to go along and perhaps help.

In order to familiarize myself with the case, I asked several questions about how long the house had been on the market, when the listing had expired, and so on. Surprisingly, Phoebe did not know the answers. It was evident that she had not done her homework.

Since there was a little time left before her scheduled meeting, I suggested that we stop at the Board Office to see if we could get more information on that listing.

Sure enough, we learned four things. The house had been on the market for five months, listed for four months, and expired for one month. A contract had been accepted during the listing period. The sale had fallen through because the buyers were unable to qualify for a mortgage. Finally, the most interesting bit of information was that the sales price of the contract was $1500 *less* than the offer Phoebe was about to present.

Of course, with this information on hand, Phoebe's whole attitude changed and so did her presentation. She did not have to be apologetic or apprehensive about the offer. Should the sellers object to the price, she was prepared to handle it. In addition, she was aware of the need to emphasize the fact that the buyers she represented were well qualified to obtain a mortgage.

As a result of knowing these few facts, Phoebe was prepared to negotiate more effectively. The sellers responded accordingly and Phoebe turned what she felt was going to be a difficult presentation into an easy acceptance.

Planning to sell a new listing

Many agents feel that they have been successful when they have the seller's signature on a listing agreement. They move on to new objectives and leave the listing to sell itself. While securing a listing is certainly a major accomplishment, no money is earned until the property is actually sold.

If you are to be prosperous and if you are to provide your client with the service you have promised, you will need to turn your attention to marketing the listing. While all of the positive features of the home are fresh in your mind, sit down and write up your brochure and two or three ads. Here are some tips:

1. Verify and include in the brochures all of the pertinent facts about the property. Omission of important details, or inclusion of inaccurate information can create problems and may lose the sale entirely.

2. Make a list of all the benefits and features, from the buyer's point of view, emphasizing those features that will attract a buyer to that particular house.

3. Condense, being careful to describe the property so that you will obtain maximum results with minimum words.

4. Keep on hand for reference a collection of impressive ads, in addition to your own which have been effective. You don't have to rely on your own creative ability to write ads that are power-pulling. I find it helpful to borrow words and phrases from others, particularly from ads for large developments or expensive homes. These are generally written by highly paid professionals who work exclusively in the advertising business. Adapting some of their words or phrases may be just the final touch you need to sell your particular listing.

Preparation—the key to a $750,000 sale

Gloria was a former student of mine. I ran into her recently at an educational seminar. She was bubbly and excited, and rightly so. Earlier that evening she had sold 28 acres for the sum of three-quarters of a million dollars.

She told me that she realized that the key to her success in this transaction was just what she had been taught—preparation. She explained that the research she had done in gathering all of the available information and in assembling it in a comprehensive fashion was responsible for sparking her buyer's interest and confidence.

The facts she submitted consisted of such things as zoning, square footage, elevation, topography (trees, farmed, or other ground cover), plat, survey, location of utilities, availability of services, aerial, roadways and access, and surrounding facilities. She claimed that she drew a complete picture instead of offering a sketch from a Multiple Listing book.

Her buyer was greatly impressed by the professional manner of her presentation, which was in marked contrast to the other proposals he had received. In fact, he was amazed at the number of salespeople who had neglected to check out some of the most important details, such as elevation or availability of sewerage, water, or electricity. According to Gloria, she was handsomely paid for her hours of preparation.

The five P's: Proper preparation prevents poor performance

"Proper preparation prevents poor performance" is a formula you can use to guarantee an increase in your efficiency and productivity. Proper preparation is the one ingredient that successful professionals have in common. If you closely observe the competent lawyer, doctor, actor, or real estate salesperson, you will notice that each one of them takes time to thoroughly prepare himself. This assures him of a top performance each time.

An important point to learn from a famous attorney

Samuel S. Leibowitz, the famous New York criminal lawyer, was once asked after winning a very difficult case, "At what point in the trial did you win this case?"

"I won the case a month before the trial opened," he responded. "When I went into the courtroom, I had the answers to every bit of evidence the District Attorney could use against me. This involved a great deal of work.

"In preparing for a trial, I make up a list of things which are against my client and then list all the things in his favor. The opposing attorney cannot surprise me with evidence to which I have no answer."

Preparation was the secret of Samuel Leibowitz's success. It can also be the secret of your success, just as it was for me in showing houses to the R.'s, for Phoebe when presenting her contract, and for Gloria in making her $750,000 sale. These are just a few examples of the results of following the five P's. You'll find that this formula will prove itself in each phase of every transaction in which you may be involved. But don't take my word for it. Why not prove it to yourself? You'll be glad you did.

Checklist for Planning a Productive Day

Do you devote a certain amount of time to plan each day's activities by:

　　Making a daily list of 12 activities?

　　Listing them in order of importance?

　　Finishing them one at a time, working from the top down?

Do you have on hand the tools you need to consummate each selling situation?

　　Use a checklist to ensure that you have all of your tools?

　　Use a prepared questionnaire to obtain complete and correct information regarding the property, seller, and buyer?

　　Prepare research material in anticipation of questions that may arise?

Do you write the brochure and two or three ads immediately after signing the listing agreement, and verify and include in the brochure all pertinent facts regarding the property?

　　Make a list of all benefits/features in a minimum number of words?

　　Condense wording for maximum results in minimum words?

　　Revise brochures/ads using language from previously successful ads?

Do you have a confident attitude about succeeding in the selling situations you planned for the day?

　　Getting the appointment?

　　Selling the seller?

　　Offering the new listing?

　　Showing the property?

　　Winning at the negotiating table?

　　Making the sale stay closed for keeps?

Do you think optimistically at all times?

2

Talking Too Much—
A Fatal Mistake!

Kathryn, a bright and experienced saleswoman, admitted that she had a bad habit of talking too much. In fact, it was one of her biggest problems and it almost cost her a sale.

Kathryn was presenting a complicated offer on one of my listings. Each time the seller asked a question, Kathryn began to answer with long, detailed explanations. I noticed that this tended to confuse and annoy him. I felt compelled to stop her in order to save the sale, so I interrupted frequently, tactfully requested brief answers, or I reworded Kathryn's answers in simple explanations. The seller became relaxed and receptive and he willingly signed the offer.

Later, Kathryn thanked me for the assistance I had given her. She was aware of what had happened, and later asked me if I had any suggestions to help her in the future to overcome her habit of talking too much.

After assuring her that she was not alone and that being overly talkative is a common mistake many real estate salespeople make, I offered her the following simple but effective suggestion.

An effective way to refrain from talking too much

Take a 3 x 5 card.

Write on it in large bold letters: *DON'T TALK TOO MUCH.*

Glance at it frequently.

Repeat the words to yourself, especially on the way to your appointment. You won't talk nearly as much, because you'll be so conscious of it during the entire interview.

Spectacular sales story

A few weeks later, Kathryn told me this story. She had a VA contract to present. At the same time, there were two others, another VA and a conventional. To her astonishment, her contract was accepted even though it was $500 less than the other VA. She was stunned and could hardly believe it.

On the way home she thought about it, wondering how and why it had happened. She reviewed the course of events. Remembering what I had told her, she had made a very conscious effort not to talk too much. Slowly and briefly, she had presented the pertinent details of the contract along with a few brief remarks about her buyers and their qualifications. The other two salespeople got very excited, raised their voices, shouted at the same time, and became argumentative, all of which seemed to harass the seller, who suddenly reached over, snatched Kathryn's contract, and hastily signed it. Needless to say, all three of them were shocked.

Kathryn was convinced that they had lost the sale by talking too much. She had won by controlling the impulse.

The most common error in selling

After a meeting of purchasing agents of General Electric, Mr. Harry Erlicher, a vice-president, remarked, "We took a vote today to find out the biggest reason why salesmen lose business. It is significant to note that the vote was three to one that salesmen talk too much."

This is particularly true of real estate salespeople. Of all the mistakes they make, talking too much is the most common and the most devastating. If you think about this and if you are honest with yourself, you'll most likely come to the conclusion that you too are frequently guilty of committing this error.

It is said, and rightly so, that a real estate salesman often talks himself into and then talks himself out of a sale or listing.

That is exactly what happened recently to Stanley, a prominent and successful Realtor.

How a listing was lost

Stanley prides himself on the fact that he is usually very careful not to get involved in side discussions. However, one evening he slipped and lost the listing.

All was going very smoothly on a listing interview in which he was accompanied by one of his new associates. Somehow the conversation drifted and Mrs. F. asked Stanley how he felt about the current topic of whether teachers should have the right to punish students. Quickly and without thinking, he responded that, yes, he thought the time had come to make students behave. It was his feeling that giving teachers the right to discipline through punishment was long overdue, and that unless some action was taken, children would realize that they could get away with misbehavior. This, he claimed, was one reason why students don't have respect for their teachers.

To his surprise, Mrs. F. stood up and angrily retorted, "Well, I don't want any teacher to dare put a hand on *my* child! I'll do the punishing, not anyone else!"

She stalked out of the room and did not return. What started out to be a very favorable listing interview ended suddenly and sadly.

Why real estate salespeople talk too much

Why do we talk so much? Some of the most common reasons include the following:

1. You've spent a great deal of time in preparation and you have learned a great deal. You therefore feel compelled to share all you have discovered.

2. You're not listening attentively. You're thinking of what to say next and you're eager to say it.

3. You may think that you'll really impress your buyers and sellers by telling them how much you know.

4. Fearing that your customer will consider you incompetent, you tend to go on and on, particularly in situations where you feel you don't have all of the information.

5. Feeling overconfident, you may chatter away incessantly.

6. Perhaps you think that they are buying too soon. You have more to tell. You can make the sale "solid," so you continue talking right past the selling point.

7. On the other hand, you may feel that you have oversold. To be sure that you leave your prospect with a good feeling, you talk on.

8. Perhaps you feel that it is your duty to be the authority, to protect and advise your clients, so you tell them what you think from your standpoint and what they should do about it.

Whatever the reason is, when you concentrate on correcting the mistake of talking too much, you will obtain many favorable results.

THE BENEFITS YOU'LL GAIN

1. You'll save a lot of time.
2. You'll stick to the main points of your presentation.
3. You'll find it easier to develop other essential selling skills, such as asking questions, listening, and closing.
4. You won't be losing sales or listings by introducing objections.
5. You'll allow your clients to talk freely and sell themselves.
6. Most importantly, you will reap the rewards of having more listings and sales.

TECHNIQUES YOU CAN USE TO GAIN THESE BENEFITS

Handling incoming telephone calls

One of the most common and serious mistakes many sales-people are guilty of making happens on incoming calls. A call comes in on an ad. To the first or perhaps the second question, the agent gives complete, lengthy details of all the fine features and benefits of that particular property. He doesn't stop for a moment. He goes on and on. Generally, this information does not even meet the caller's requirements, but the agent hasn't stopped to find that out. Finally, when the caller (who might have been a good prospect) can get a word in edgewise, the response will probably be, "Thank you, but no thank you!" followed by a dial tone. Does this sound familiar?

Because the salesman did all the talking, asked no questions, and learned nothing about the caller, he lost the opportunity to gain a prospect for a sale.

The technique that works well with incoming calls is to answer each question with a qualifying question in order to learn exactly what the caller desires. If the response to your question indicates that a particular specification does not meet the caller's requirements, then there is no need to continue describing that particular property. Note this example:

Caller: "What is the price of that house?"

Agent: "They are asking $79,500. Is that the price you are interested in?"

Caller: "No, we want something at about $50,000 or possibly $55,000."

At this point, you should stop talking about this house and start asking questions for further specifications, what the caller has in mind, what he wants and needs. Arrange for an appointment to show $50,000 to $60,000 homes accordingly. Here is another illustration:

Caller: "Is there room for a pool?"

Agent: "No, there isn't enough room for a pool. Is a pool important to you and your family?"

Caller: "Yes, that is the one thing we must have."

The caller has confirmed a strong desire for a pool. Since the house she called about does not have a pool, and since there isn't room to accommodate one, there's no need to continue telling her about the merits of this house. Go no further in that direction, but continue questioning to find out what other specifications are important to her and her family. Arrange to show houses that will match these requirements.

How talking too much introduces objections— a case in point

After an interview, if you take time to review what went wrong and when it happened, you will probably discover that nearly every objection that came up was the result of something you, in your eagerness, had previously introduced. At the time, no doubt, you thought you were just contributing some additional information, but instead it cropped up later as an objection.

Ed H., an enthusiastic salesman, ran into this problem when he was showing some "hot" buyers through a lovely home. As they approached the kitchen, they spotted the oven. He thought that everyone would appreciate this modern convenience. Ed told them at great length all about the wonderful benefits of a self-cleaning oven and how it worked. His buyers listened politely. When Ed finished, the husband responded, "Oh, no! My wife hates self-cleaning ovens. She can't stand them."

When Ed was asked, "Is that a self-cleaning oven?" he should have answered simply, "Yes." Before volunteering the merits of a self-cleaning oven, Ed could have checked by asking questions, such as, "How do you feel about self-cleaning ovens? Do you like them?" He would have known right away that it was not wise to pursue the matter further.

Learn to be brief—the folly of telling it all

How tempting it is to tell all you have learned, especially after you have spent many hours in preparation. Don't allow yourself to fall into that trap. If you do, you will run the risk of losing sales and listings. You prepared thoroughly just in case you might need the answers, but some of the questions will never come up.

Determine first whether more information is needed before volunteering all you know, just because you know. Draw from your storage of information only if, when, and whatever is necessary. Always remind yourself to be brief.

The preceding two cases are examples of the dangers of not being brief. At the negotiating table, Kathryn wanted to give lengthy details, irritated the seller, and nearly lost the sale. When Ed was asked a simple question about the oven, he annoyed his buyers and made an issue of it by answering with an unnecessary dissertation.

Saving the ammunition

In each selling situation, having done your research, you may feel that you are well-equipped with the proper solutions to the problems involved. Why not cover all bases now and wrap it up quickly? Things usually don't work out that way. Doubts and delays often set in, causing the prospect to hesitate.

Instead of giving the complete presentation, try placing some of the strong selling points in reserve. Wait, and when the prospect hesitates in making the final favorable decision, or when all seems lost, use these points to rekindle the fire.

Introduce these saved up ideas in a casual manner, prefacing them with such phrases as, "By the way ... ," or, "In addition ... ," or, "I forgot to mention ... ," or, "Here's something else to consider ... "

The strong selling point or inducement that you hold in reserve can keep your sale from slipping and at the same time can spark renewed interest. It prevents procrastinating, and it can be dynamite—the very thing to clinch your listing or sale.

How the sale was clinched

My buyers saw a house one night which they liked. They wanted to go back the next morning to see it in the daylight. They still liked it and were now prepared to buy, but first they wanted their attorney to look over the contract at 5:00 that evening. This would be too late. Any delay could cause problems, including losing the house altogether or even the possibility that the prospects would change their minds. This was the ideal time to offer an inducement for them to act now. I was holding some ammunition in reserve.

It was then 11:00 a.m. In a casual manner, I explained that while I did not mind waiting until the evening, they ought to know that there was a great danger in doing so. They might sacrifice the opportunity to buy this house, the one they really loved. It was then that I told them about my conversation earlier that morning with the listing agent. The agent had told me that he was presenting a contract on that house at 1:00 and, if I had a contract as well, he'd present it at the same time. When the buyers heard this, they agreed to call their attorney at once, read the details of the contract to him (it was a standard form contract with no special terms), got his approval and signed it. I was back at the house at exactly 1:00 and was fortunately able to get our contract accepted.

I could have told the buyers about the contract as soon as we got there. Had I done so it would have been wasted. They would probably have thought I was urging them to make a quick decision. They would have resented it and resisted automatically. However, it was effective to hold off telling them until they announced a reason for delaying. Saving this information for the opportune moment made the necessary impact. It worked—they acted promptly.

Learn the powerful pause technique

The pause technique is most effective, difficult to develop, and requires a great deal of practice. But it works very well in two situations. The first occurs when your buyer or seller asks you a question. Even though you know the answer, you hesitate, delaying a moment or two before answering. You *pause*. This gives you two advantages:

1. It feeds the ego of your buyer or seller. He feels that he has asked an important, intelligent question, perhaps one to which you may not know the answer.
2. It gives you time to:
   a) Collect your thoughts in order to give the best possible answer.
   b) Plan your next question, designed to lead his thinking in a favorable direction.

In the second situation, the greater power of the pause can be felt if used properly. When this technique is used following a closing question, it is truly potent. First, you ask a closing question, such as, "What do you think of this house?" or, "Are you interested in assuming the existing mortgage?" or, "You would want us to get the highest price for your home, wouldn't you?" Then you pause. You remain absolutely silent. You wait for an answer. Although it may be only moments, it will seem like much longer. The silence will seem endless. Meanwhile, ideas about what you want to say next will be racing through your mind and you'll be tempted to introduce a new point. Don't do it! Wait. The response to your question is very valuable. It reveals where you stand in your presentation. The answer is the clue, either consent to buy or an excuse for not buying now. Of course, if the response is consent to buy, stop talking and start writing the agreement. If, on the other hand, you get an excuse, get right back on the track and continue selling.

A word of caution: To get the maximum benefit from this technique, make certain that you pause for long enough to allow your client or customer to speak his mind *completely*—not merely one or two sentences. Otherwise, you may never learn what might be the most important part of his reaction to your question. Too often, the salesman either does not wait long enough to get the full response, or, in his anxiety to sell, he starts to talk too soon.

As I mentioned before, this technique of pausing may be difficult to develop, but it pays off well when you practice it.

The pause that produced surprising results

John had shown Mrs. P. three houses. Two of them seemed to John to be what she was looking for, because she had stressed the fact that the house must be clean and neat so that she could move right in. He thought that one home in particular was ideal. Was she ready to make a decision? He wasn't quite sure. To test her, he asked a closing question: "Which of the three houses do you like the best?"

John waited patiently for her answer, all the time thinking of what he would say next. He was tempted to embellish on the merits of the one house he felt was right for her. But he remained silent. Mrs. P. deliberated, John said nothing, and the waiting seemed endless. Then came Mrs. P.'s surprising response: "Although I did say I wanted a house that was clean and wouldn't require any work, I like the third house the best. It's minutes away from my work. That will be a great convenience for me. Although the other houses are in excellent condition, I'll arrange to get this one painted, cleaned, and fixed up before I move in. Since it is vacant, perhaps the seller might be willing to permit me to start doing it ahead of time. Do you think that is possible?"

Her answer following the pause indicated that she had bought the third house—much to John's astonishment. By not talking, by waiting patiently and listening to her complete answer, John was indeed surprised to discover that Mrs. P. was not only ready to buy but she chose the house he had least expected her to like.

Other harmful habits of talking too much

Since your aim is to win buyers and sellers, not to antagonize them, you'll want to avoid any bad habits arising from talking too much. The following are a few more habits that turn people off.

Interrupting. You may be eager to get your next point across, so without realizing it you interrupt the other person. To most people this is very annoying. On the other hand, if you let them have *their* full say, you'll find that they will often sell themselves.

Arguing. You can win the argument, but chances are you'll

lose the sale. As the late Senator Hubert Humphrey once said in a television interview, "I find you can win when you lose."

Not paying attention to everything they say. When you are doing all the talking, you aren't listening to what the other person is saying. People find this disturbing, annoying, and frustrating. In addition, you are the loser because you cheat yourself out of the opportunity to note the important things they have to tell you that might lead to finalizing the sale.

Repeating certain words. "Uh-huh, uh-huh"; "yeah! yeah!"; "see? see?"; "get me? get me?"; "you know! you know!"; "O.K.! O.K.!" This is an easy habit to get into. But once you are conscious of doing it, you will no doubt make an effort to correct this distracting habit.

To sum up this chapter, let me say again that any mistake can cost you a sale or a listing, but there is none more serious or deadly than talking too much. If you follow these guidelines and use these techniques, you'll be pleased with the results. You will both improve your performance records and increase your income.

Checklist for Overcoming Talking Too Much

Do you avoid talking too much by keeping a card that reads, "Don't talk too much," in front of you while dealing with clients, or just keeping the phrase in mind?

> Answer a caller's question with a question to find out more about what the caller is looking for?

> Only offer applicable information, not all that you know on the subject?

> Save a few strong points in reserve to use in closing?

> Pause before answering your client's questions, after asking a closing question, and long enough to let your client answer completely?

> Refrain from saying some things that later might come back as objections?

Do you avoid habits which turn clients off, such as

> Interrupting?

> Arguing?

> Not paying attention to everything your clients say?

> Repeating words like "O.K.," "uh-huh," "you know"?

3

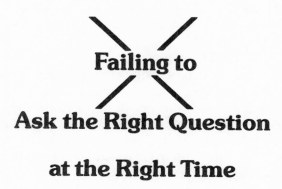

Failing to

Ask the Right Question

at the Right Time

**How the right question at the right time made
an unbelievable sale unbelievably fast**

One Saturday morning, a call came in to me about an ad. As
is often the case, this particular house did not meet the caller's
requirements.

"What I need," Mrs. S. said, "is a three bedroom, two bath
house, between $40,000 and $45,000, east of the highway, in the
Palmetto High School district, with a high mortgage that I can
assume." I didn't think this would be very difficult.

But then she added, "And I must be in by Wednesday." This
complicated matters a bit. It meant finding a house with a high
assumable mortgage that was also vacant.

After checking the Multiple Listings, I called her back to tell
her she was in luck. There was just one house that seemed to fulfill
all of her requirements. I asked her when during that afternoon she
would like to see it.

Much to my astonishment, she replied, "Oh! I can't go today.
In fact, it's impossible for me to get there before Tuesday."

I wondered if she was serious, and whether this would just be a wild goose chase.

The next carefully posed question not only gave me the answer, but made me feel that there was a possibility that I could accomplish the impossible. It was worth a try.

"Mrs. S., may I ask you one more question? If you see this house on Tuesday, and if it does suit your needs and is just what you want, can you buy it in your own name alone, or must you get your husband's approval?"

"Oh, no! My husband does not have to see it. This is my second marriage and I will be using my own money."

This response revealed that she was serious. It was also an admission that she could and would perform on her own if she liked the house. She had committed herself and was mentally conditioned to take action at once. Her answer to this closing question indicated to me that there was a real possibility of a quick sale. It was certainly worth pursuing.

We set up the appointment for Tuesday morning at 10:30. Because we were coming from opposite directions, each traveling about 20 miles, we met at the house in order to save time.

Mrs. S. saw the house, liked it, made an offer, called the movers at 4:00 p.m., put deposits on the utilities, and was in the house on Wednesday, the next day.

It really did happen. Of course, since the seller was out of town, we were fortunate enough to reach him by phone, negotiate on terms and price, and get an agreement on a two-week rental arrangement. But what seemed to be improbable and almost impossible did occur. "Can you buy this house in your name alone?" was the key question in making this unbelievable sale.

THE BENEFITS YOU'LL GAIN

1. You'll have time to think.
2. You'll probe to discover the needs, wants, feelings, reactions, and motivations of your buyer and seller.
3. You'll feed their egos and maintain their interest.
4. You'll avoid the mistake of talking too much because you won't be telling, you'll be asking.
5. You'll seek their opinions instead of offering yours.
6. You'll be inquiring, not jumping to conclusions.

7. You'll control the conversation.

8. You'll be able to gently guide your clients to a favorable decision. You'll be aware of when they are ready to close.

9. Finally, you'll make more money by asking the right questions than by knowing the right answers.

Selling isn't telling—it's asking

One can usually recognize a professional salesperson by the way he directs and leads the thinking of his prospects. This is accomplished through the skillful use of questions. From the beginning, he uses a series of fact-finding questions combined with closing questions. He may start with, "If we find just what you are looking for, are you prepared to make the decision today?" Then he continues with more questioning throughout the entire interview, including asking for the order to buy or sell, which he does frequently. In other words, the professional doesn't *tell;* he *asks.*

In the previous chapter, I described how telling can be harmful to a sale. The opposite of *telling* is *asking,* and that can surely be beneficial. So, in this chapter I'll examine some of the various types of questions to show you when and how you can use them effectively.

TECHNIQUES YOU CAN USE TO GAIN THESE BENEFITS

Answer a question with a question

1. *When they ask a question:* When a buyer or a seller asks a question, the agent is often anxious to reply immediately. Regardless of whether you know the answer or not, it is more advantageous not to answer too quickly. When you hesitate, it makes the other person feel smart, and he thinks that he has asked a good question. Then you can reply with a question such as, "Is that important to you?" or, "Why do you ask?" or, "Before I answer you, Mr. Prospect, I want to make sure I understand your question. Do you mean ... ?"

When you answer with a question, you'll be able to:

- Answer the question correctly by clarifying it.
- Collect your thoughts for a good answer, rather than saying the first thing that comes to mind.
- Think of what to say next so you can control and determine the

direction of the interview. As Socrates said, "He who asks questions has command."

2. *Ask them first:* Replying to a question by asking for the prospect's views first is a method that works well. Too often, we assume that they are asking because they approve, or we assume that they like a home or a feature because we do. How much wiser it is to confirm an opinion instead of taking it for granted.

For example, the prospect may spot a fireplace and ask, "Is that a wood-burning fireplace?" You would answer, "Yes, it is. How do you feel about wood-burning fireplaces? Do you like them?" The answer, of course, indicates the prospect's true views, which can influence your tactics accordingly.

You may recall the story of Stanley in the previous chapter. That was a simple illustration of the importance of first asking how the other person feels before answering his question. Stanley would have avoided Mrs. F.'s wrath if he had first asked her how *she* felt about whether teachers should have the right to punish students. His reply to her question could have been, "What are your feelings about it, Mrs. F.?" Then he would have learned her opinion before volunteering his opposing views, and he could have saved the listing.

3. *Answering with a question to close:* Turning the prospect's question into a closing question is another useful technique. For instance:

Buyer: "Do all the appliances stay?"

Agent: "Do you want the appliances to stay?"

Buyer: "Could we be in the house within a month?"

Agent: "Would you want to be in the house within a month?"

Buyer: "Do the draperies and carpeting stay?"

Agent: "Do you want the draperies and carpeting to stay?"

If the buyer answers positively, it indicates that he already sees himself in the house, and he has virtually bought it.

How and when to ask open-ended questions

An "open-ended question" is any question that cannot be answered with a simple "yes" or "no." These questions probe and produce the keys to discovering the facts, feelings, and motivations of the other person. They prevent one from jumping to wrong conclusions. In addition, they serve as an aid in controlling the conversation and in closing. Generally, the questions begin with some plain, popular, yet potent words. Here are seven such words: How? What? Where? When? Who? Which? Why?

The following examples illustrate this approach:

- *"How* did you arrive at the amount you are asking for your home?"
- *"What* do you think about this idea?"
- *"When* would you like to move in?"
- *"Who* else will have to be consulted?"
- *"Which* of these floor plans do you like best?"
- *"Why* do you hesitate?"

You use these kinds of questions all the time, in every conversation. To get the best results, you must remember to practice the pause after asking each question, as discussed in the previous chapter.

Using tie-downs to get your buyer or seller nodding in agreement

Throughout your presentation, you will find it very effective to use questions that produce a series of commitments. For this specific purpose, you can use a highly professional technique called the "tie-down."

You make a positive statement, then immediately add a question which compels the other person to agree with you. He thus commits himself affirmatively; he is tied down.

Like most other selling techniques, this requires constant practice until it becomes automatic. However, once you develop the use of tie-down questions, you will discover what an excellent method it is for leading the thinking of your buyers or sellers to produce affirmative responses. Once they start agreeing with you on minor matters, they become conditioned. It almost becomes a habit, so they generally continue to agree all the way to the final agreement to buy, sell, or list. And that, of course, is exactly what you want.

Fred, one of the best sales managers I have ever known, used to say, "If you get your prospect nodding up and down and giving yes answers, it isn't easy for him to suddenly change to shaking his head no in the opposite direction." Listed below are some tie-downs and a few examples of how you can use them to get your clients to nod in agreement.

Wouldn't it?	Doesn't it?
Won't they?	Can't you?
Couldn't it?	Aren't you?
Isn't it?	Haven't they?
Didn't you?	Won't you?
Don't you agree?	Isn't that so?

- "It would be great to be in and settled down before school starts, *wouldn't it?*"
- "This is a very attractive mortgage rate of interest, *isn't it?*"
- "Being close in like this could solve your transportation problem, *couldn't it?*"
- "The owners have kept the house in excellent condition, *haven't they?*"

A word of caution: Don't use tie-downs if there is any doubt about the response. Use them only when you know that the answer will be affirmative. After all, you are seeking only "yes" answers, *aren't you?*

A few more ways to use questions

The "alternate-choice question" is another effective method you can use to guide your prospect toward a decision. Unlike the tie-down question, the alternate-choice question cannot be answered with a simple "yes" or "no." Yet, by the same token, the answer does indicate that the other person is prepared to go ahead. This type of question gives your buyer or seller a choice between two alternatives. Here are some samples:

- "Is tomorrow *morning* or *afternoon* more convenient to preview your home?"
- "Do you want to be *close in* or *farther out?*"
- "What is your preference—a *new* home or an *older* one?"
- "Will you assume the *existing* mortgage or apply for a *new* mortgage?"
- "Which will be more beneficial to you—a *30-* or a *60-*day closing?"

A specific example of using this type of questioning is the following:

Alternate Question: "Would you use this room as a *den* or a *bedroom?*"

Prospect: "I'd like it as a *den,* an informal room where my husband and I could comfortably relax."

or

Prospect: "We would use it as a fourth *bedroom.* That way, each child could have his own room."

As you can see, it doesn't matter which choice the prospect makes. Either way, you've made a sale.

Even though it isn't easy for him to do so, your prospect might surprise you by not choosing either answer. But this is not likely to happen if you have been getting commitments as you went along. However, if it happens, you can note his negative reaction as a valuable clue to his thinking.

Asking for the order

Right along, the questions you have been asking have been for one purpose, and that is to get the signed order. To get it, you must ask for it. Even your prospect expects you to ask. There is no special time to do this, but as the professional salesperson does, you should keep asking all the time, from the beginning of every interview through to the end. You may start with something like this: "Mr. and Mrs. Prospect, if we find a house today that you like and that meets all of your requirements, are you ready to buy it?"

Then continue with questions like the following:

- *"Do you* have anything else in mind that you would like included?"

- *"Supposing* the seller insists on a 30-day closing, *are you* prepared to go along with that?"

- *"Will you* please write your name here exactly as it is written on the first line?"

The phrase "what if" is especially potent when you are asking for the order:

- *"What if* I am able to get the seller to take back a small second mortgage on this house. *Will you* buy it?"

- *"What if* I can convince the buyers to purchase the house as is. *Would you* accept this price?"

- *"What if* I can get the seller to adjust the price to take care of the painting. *Could you* do the painting yourself?"

- *"What if* I could get the owner to include the freezer and the workbench and the cabinets in the garage. *Will you* buy this house?"

A good rule to follow

Before leaving, ask one more time, "Mr. and Mrs. Buyer, may I ask if there is truly any reason why you shouldn't buy this house right now?" Or, "Mr. and Mrs. Seller, may I ask if there is really any reason why you shouldn't employ me right now to represent you as your agent in selling your house?"

You have now followed the professional salesperson's basic rule of continually asking for the order. When you do this, don't be surprised if nine out of ten times you do get exactly what you have asked for.

How I got a "hot" listing

Earlier, I told you how asking the right question at the right time made a sale. Let me tell you about a very "hot" listing that was obtained in the same way.

The house showed like a "model," immaculate and attractively decorated. It was located in a very desirable, rather recent development. The D.'s were being transferred. They had to be in their new location within the month. What more could any real estate agent want? It was a beautiful house, in a choice location, with a motivated seller, and even a realistic price.

Real estate agents were calling constantly. Mrs. D. told everyone, "We've sold all of our previous homes by ourselves and we intend to do the same now. Even if we don't sell it, my husband's company will take it off our hands. We aren't interested in talking to any real estate agents." This, of course, discouraged most of the agents.

When I stopped by to view the house anyway and chat with Mrs. D., she told me again how adamant her husband was about not talking to any Realtors. But then she confided that she wished she could get Mr. D. to talk to some Realtors now. It would be so much easier for her if she didn't have the responsibility at this time, since she had so much else to do.

I offered, "Mrs. D., I believe I can help you. I have an idea. *Will you be willing to try it?* Tell your husband we had a pleasant visit and that I suggested that he just hear about what services are available to him, if and when he might decide to seek the assistance of a Realtor. Be sure to explain that there will be absolutely no obligation on his part now or in the future. Do you think you'd be willing to try this idea?"

She agreed to give it a try, but she was sure it wouldn't work, because her husband was very stubborn about this matter.

Not only did I have the opportunity to meet and talk with Mr. D. that very night, but I was pleasantly surprised very early in the interview by his asking what the commission fee would be and then signing the agreement. That super listing was mine, and very easily, too.

Mrs. D. later told me that she was bombarded with calls from real estate agents who were wondering how it all happened so fast. Asking the question, *"I have an idea, will you try it?"* worked wonders, and the house sold within two weeks.

Ask—ask—ask

I've given you just two examples of how asking the right question at the right time brought good results: one listing, one sale. If you will follow the techniques of asking questions in each of the eight specific situations discussed in Chapter 1—from making appointments to processing the sale—you too will discover that there is more money to be made from asking the right question than from knowing the right answer.

A point to ponder

Why not add the words, "Ask Questions," to the 3 x 5 reminder card suggested in Chapter 2? Your card will now read:

```
Don't Talk Too Much
Ask Questions
```

Checklist for Making Good Use of Questions

Do you combine fact-finding and closing questions?

Do you ask rather than tell?

Do you answer a question with a question?

    Find out the reason behind the question?

    Give a thoughtful answer?

    Direct and control the conversation?

Do you ask open-ended questions at every chance?

    Use *how, when, where, who, which, why*?

    Avoid assuming?

Do you get plenty of commitments?

    Change a positive statement into a more positive commitment?

Do you use questions to improve your selling effectiveness?

    Force a definite decision by giving your prospect a choice between one thing and something else?

    Find out why the prospect didn't buy?

    Continuously and creatively ask for the order?

4

Not

Mastering the Most Important

Real Estate Selling Skill—

The Art of Listening

Of all the mistakes a real estate salesperson makes, not listening and talking too much are probably the two most serious and common ones. Listening is one of the most rewarding skills a real estate salesperson can develop. In fact, the top producers themselves will tell you that much of their success is due to their ability to listen effectively to their buyers and sellers.

In the first three chapters, I covered some of the techniques that are essential for successful selling: preparation, not talking too much, and asking questions. However, even if you were conscientious and diligent in your preparation, even if you were careful not to talk too much, and even if you made certain to ask many questions, even if you did all these things, you would still stand the chance of losing the listing or sale if you failed to listen effectively to the other person.

What does it mean to listen?

First, I'll explain specifically what listening means. The dictionary tells us that to *listen* means "to make a conscious effort to hear; to hear with thoughtful attention."

But listening is even more than that. It's a behavioral skill, an art, a discipline. It's both mental and physical. It draws on all of your senses. It requires a great deal of effort, self-control, and complete concentration.

How listening affects you—a case in point

In his book, *My Life In Court,* lawyer Louis Nizer claims that when a hostile witness is testifying, his concentration is so complete that at the end of a day in court in which he has only listened, he finds himself wringing wet despite his calm and composed manner. During every trial, Mr. Nizer says he loses from two to ten pounds.

Listening effectively is an enormous strain. Since the ability to listen is not an inborn trait, you do have to work hard in order to develop this important skill.

THE BENEFITS YOU'LL GAIN

1. You'll save time. When you listen the first time, you won't have to go back the second time for clarification. Since time is a salesperson's asset, any time you can save is valuable.
2. You'll flatter your buyers and sellers. They'll love the opportunity to have someone listen to them and their problems.
3. You'll engage in a true dialogue. When people sense that they have your undivided attention, they'll be at ease and talk freely.
4. You'll establish good communication. From your exclusive attention, your clients will realize that you care and are concerned about them.
5. You'll earn your clients' trust and confidence.
6. You'll learn a lot. You'll pick up pieces of information that you'll be glad to have.
7. You'll observe movements which silently say many things.
8. You'll perceive your prospects' thinking. When you digest what they reveal about themselves, you'll know what they really want and need.

9. You'll filter out and store in your memory bank both negative and positive reactions.
10. You won't be assuming or jumping to conclusions when you weigh what the speaker is saying or doing. You'll discern the meanings of his words and actions.
11. You won't miss anything important. When you're paying close attention to the subject at hand, your mind won't wander.
12. You'll notice the buying signals. When you listen attentively, you'll pick up the clues that prospects drop which indicate that they are ready to buy or sell.
13. You'll let your clients sell themselves. They like to do this but can't if you do the talking and they do the listening.
14. And, of course, you'll make the most of each selling situation. The result will be more properties listed and sold than you ever had before.

TECHNIQUES YOU CAN USE TO GAIN THESE BENEFITS

Stop! Look! Listen! The railroads used to have these signs posted at all their crossings, as a warning that a train might be approaching. Even though the signs are no longer there, everyone is still aware of how valid those words are. Your life might depend on your coming to a complete *stop, looking* in both directions, and *listening* carefully to hear if a train is approaching. This ensures a safe crossing.

You might wisely heed this same warning as you approach the various crossroads of selling real estate. If you do, you'll find that you can save, not kill, your sale.

First, *stop* talking. Give the other person the floor. From Chapter 2, you already know how vital this is to any sale.

Second, *look* directly at your prospect. Keep your eyes focused on him. His facial expression may reveal some things that his lips won't. Naturally, the more you know about what he is thinking, the easier it is for you to guide him.

Third, *listen* carefully. This does not mean to pretend, but it does mean giving an ear, your undivided attention. When you practice these three success secrets, you'll be well on your way to safely reaching your destination, a sale.

HOW TO LISTEN EFFECTIVELY

Realizing the difference between hearing and listening

Hearing and listening are not the same, and while many real estate salespeople seem to think these two words are synonymous, they are really quite different. Hearing is passive, while listening is active. When a person is speaking, you may hear the sound, the voice, and the words, but you are not actually listening, unless you pay thoughtful attention to the meaning of the speaker's words and actions.

A common tale of woe

One day an agent in my real estate class was nodding her head up and down and smiling as we discussed the fact that many agents do not listen closely to what the buyers say they want and need. When buyers have to go out day after day looking at homes which are not what they specified, they become annoyed, disappointed, and frustrated. Julia, the student, said, "That's exactly what happened to me." She told us how she had moved to Miami from up north and was anxious to get settled. Every day for a week she went out with the same agent. And every day Julia carefully repeated the same specifications of what she was looking for. Yet, each day the salesperson seemed to pay no attention at all to what Julia was telling her, continuing to show her homes that did not suit her needs. Finally, Julia was disgusted, discouraged, and desperate, and she ended up finding a house by herself.

Julia concluded that if the salesperson had only listened, she would have made the sale and made Julia a happy, satisfied customer.

From this simple illustration, you can readily see that there is a vast difference between hearing the words and listening to them. Because listening involves not only receiving but also digesting and mentally recording the messages the speaker is sending, it is essential that you follow the next step in developing the art of listening—concentrating.

Concentrating

To concentrate, you obliterate everything from your mind and give total attention to whatever is being said. You clear your mind of other thoughts in order to 1) focus your attention on the speaker and the subject at hand, 2) completely absorb what you hear, 3) prevent your mind from wandering, 4) try not to miss anything important, 5) retain information to use to clinch the sale.

Complete concentration entails specific straining. While you're paying exclusive attention to the speaker, you are at the same time trying to understand what is being said as you mentally sift, sort, and record information. In other words, while you are weighing what the speaker is saying, your mind is also acting as a human computer, storing data in your memory bank for recall when you may need it.

Such effort is hard work and requires plenty of practice. It drains you both mentally and physically, as was evident in the case of Mr. Nizer, the lawyer mentioned earlier. You may recall that he tells what a strain it is for him when he concentrates on listening at trials. Nevertheless, when you work at developing the ability to concentrate while listening, it will definitely be worth the effort and very rewarding. In fact, acquiring the ability to concentrate will contribute toward the success of future sales.

Showing your clients that you want to listen

As a result of your experience, knowledge, and research, you no doubt feel that you have much to share. In order to listen effectively, however, you must forego being the advisor and instead permit the other person to have the stage. This, of course, means that you subordinate your own ego and remain silent. In order to do this, you need to be patient, permissive, and to look directly at the speaker. It isn't enough just to look at your buyer or seller; you must also act interested in what is being said. If, on the other hand, you only pretend to listen, they'll know that you are not sincere or concerned about them and their problems, and they'll be turned off.

By refraining from doing what comes naturally—namely, telling instead of listening—you successfully feed the other person's ego. This will pay off in various ways. It puts your prospects at ease, encourages them to speak their minds freely and frankly, while revealing their true feelings. And, ultimately, you'll be surprised at what valuable information you'll be obtaining.

Asking questions to show you are listening

To denote further interest, illustrate that you care, perceive significant points, and prevent the other person from rambling, you can ask questions, as in Chapter 3. Then you should wait and really listen to the answers. After all, if you don't pay attention to the answers, what's the use of asking the questions in the first place? The buyers will complain, saying that real estate agents ask them what they want and then totally ignore what they tell them.

So, to avoid misunderstandings, and to indicate that you're listening to what is being said, here are some sample questions you can use:

- "Can you clarify this for me?"
- "Do you mean ... ?"
- "I understand. Will you consider ... ?"
- "To make sure I understand exactly what you want, will you please go over the details you have given me thus far?"

Listening with your eyes

Master salespeople realize that there is more to watch for and listen to than just the spoken words. They witness the fact that actions do often speak louder than words. The idea is to take particular notice of the messages being sent by nonverbal communication, commonly referred to as body language.

You can do this by observing your prospect's facial expressions and his actions. You may become aware of some very important feelings your prospect may never voice. You'll be amazed at what you will detect when you listen with your eyes as well as your ears.

Watching for gestures—what they will tell you

When you are listening with your eyes, the following are some common body movements you'll see and what they silently say:

- A frown: "I'm puzzled. I don't understand. I'm confused. Please explain."
- Pulling back, stepping back, looking away: "I'm disinterested, annoyed, offended."
- Rubbing eyes, shifting restlessly, a yawn: "I'm tired, bored, impatient."
- Moving closer, picking up brochure or contract: "I'm interested, convinced, ready to go."
- A nod: "I like it. I agree. I want it."
- Shaking the head: "No, I don't agree."

In addition, you'll want to look and listen for such important closing clues as lingering in a particular room, whispering together, privately figuring on paper. These, of course, tell you that your prospects are seriously considering buying or selling. On the other hand, when you are showing a house and the prospective buyers rush hurriedly through the house, this is generally the clue for you to move on quickly to the next house and forget about this one.

Hearing and heeding buying signals

A buying signal indicates that your prospect is ready to buy. In other words, the prospect sees himself as the owner of the property being presented or as the subscriber to the listing service being offered, and denotes this by either verbal or nonverbal signs. Since I have already covered some of the nonverbal signs, let's take a look now at some typical examples of verbal buying signals:

- "It seems to me our dining room set will fit in perfectly."
- "Of course, we could redecorate to our taste."
- "How long did you say it takes to get downtown from here?"
- "I like the idea of buying this house as an investment instead of just paying rent."
- "If I accept this price of $71,500, how much cash will I come out with?"
- "If I should decide on having a Realtor handle the selling of my house, how long would it take to get it on Multiple Listing?"

Sometimes, when you're not paying attention, you may not notice some common buying signals, such as:

- "Let's take another look at the kitchen."
- "Do you think that the master bedroom will accommodate all of our bedroom pieces?"
- "I don't like being tied up for six months."
- "If I were to give you the listing ... ?"
- "If we should decide on this house ... ?"

And, of course, if you're listening, you'll hear and heed when one spouse says to the other, "What do you think, dear?" which translates to mean, "I'm sold and ready to go. Are you, too?"

Whenever you do observe any facial expression or body movement that indicates the reaction of your buyer or seller, don't ignore or overlook it. *Stop, Look, and Listen*—either take advantage of it if it is a positive sign, or take steps to remedy it if it happens to be a negative one.

How listening and remembering one fact made it possible for a buyer to qualify for a mortgage on a $65,000 home

Sometime ago, we had sold Mr. and Mrs. N.'s house, and they were now excited about buying a more spacious home that they had found. It was on an acre, with a pool, for $65,000.

When it was time to apply for the mortgage, I accompanied Mrs. N. to the lending institution. (Her husband, who worked for an airline, was out of town.) The loan officer jotted down all of the information, including their combined incomes of $33,000. (Hers, as a surgical nurse, was $18,000.) They had two children, ages 8 and 12. This was during a time when most lending institutions were not counting the wife's salary if she was of child-bearing age. The loan officer merely said that her salary would not be counted, giving no reason, and that he did not think her husband's salary would be sufficient to qualify for the loan. It was at this point that I discovered the importance of listening, first listening to my prospect and now paying attention to the loan officer's calculations. So I volunteered, "There should be no problem. Mr. and Mrs. N.'s two children are adopted. They can't have children of their own." That did it. Her salary was, of course, included and there was no further problem or doubt about their qualifying.

Later, Mrs. N. remarked how surprised she was that I knew about the children being adopted. Not many people knew. She did not remember ever having told me, and it also would never have occurred to her to mention this fact to the loan officer.

It is significant to note that Mrs. N. had mentioned the adoption of the children only casually one day while we were house-hunting. Because I listened, stored the fact in my memory bank, and recalled it at the crucial moment, I was able to save the sale.

This case is just one example of how you can pick up some little piece of information through listening which can prove important to a sale—even when you least expect it.

Another point to ponder

Because it is difficult for most real estate salespeople to remember to control their speech muscles so that they won't talk too much, to ask questions and to listen carefully, I'd like to add the word *listen* to the reminder card I suggested at the end of Chapter 3. Since these three basic skills do require a tremendous amount of practice until they become habitual, you will find it helpful to keep your reminder card handy and glance at it frequently, especially as you prepare yourself for various selling situations. Your 3 x 5 card will now read:

```
Don't Talk Too Much
    Ask Questions
       Listen
```

Since the primary purpose of listening effectively is to obtain and retain information that can lead to a sale, I'd like to wrap up this enormously important chapter by repeating that most significant word: SALE.

Stop talking.

Ask questions.

Listen effectively.

End with a signed order.

Checklist for Listening Effectively

Do you listen effectively by:

Stopping talking?

Looking directly at your prospect?

Listening to the meanings of your prospect's words and actions?

Clearing your mind of other thoughts and

- Focusing your attention on the speaker and the subject?
- Completely absorbing what you hear?

- Preventing your mind from wandering?
- Trying not to miss anything important?
- Retaining information to use to clinch the sale?

Asking certain questions which show you're listening?

Paying attention to the answers?

Do you listen with your eyes for nonverbal messages?

Negative gestures?

Positive closing clue gestures?

Do you hear and heed verbal buying signals?

Comments and/or questions indicating interest in performing?

5

Failing to
Use Feedback Advantageously

Instinctively, you feel that your buyers were favorably impressed with the property you have just shown them. You were careful not to talk too much and listened intently to their answers to many questions. You are confident that you did a good job. Their favorable comments also confirm this. You recognize signals that seem to say, "Now is the time. We are ready."

But suddenly there seems to be a turnabout in their attitude. They are wavering; they've become fearful and indecisive. What do you do next?

It is at such times that the star salesperson resorts to using a highly successful technique called "feedback." This effective method involves "playing back" something your buyer or seller has said.

THE BENEFITS YOU'LL GAIN

1. You'll clear the air of misunderstandings. You'll be certain to clarify so that you will really know and understand what your buyers and sellers have told you.

2. You'll help to crystallize their thoughts and avoid confusion.

3. You'll assist your prospects in arriving at a definite, favorable decision when fear and hesitation set in.

4. You'll turn objections into reasons to buy *now.* What seem to be objections are often merely excuses which, when you use feedback, can be converted into the very reasons why they should go ahead.

5. You'll give them the happy, satisfied feeling that they *bought* and were not *sold.* People like to think they made up their own minds.

TECHNIQUES YOU CAN USE TO GAIN THESE BENEFITS

Overcoming hesitation

It is part of human nature to become hesitant just before making a final decision. A prospect wonders, "Am I doing the right thing? Should I delay in making a decision now? Should I look further? What will my friends and family say?" What your prospect really means is, "Won't you please help me, reassure me that if I go ahead today I'll be doing the right thing? I don't want to make a mistake."

What better way is there to reassure and reinforce the customer's feelings than by letting him hear once again something he previously said about the property in question. This is an ideal time for you to use feedback by repeating and reminding him of some of the specifics you carefully listened to when you qualified him, and the positive comments he made when he toured the house.

Let's take a simple example. Mr. and Mrs. J. stressed the fact that they wanted to be close to Mr. J.'s office. They did not want to be on a busy street, however, and they wanted some seclusion. When they saw the house, both Mr. and Mrs. J. "oohed" and "aahed" over the yard, where they lingered for a while. They expressed their love for gardening and an interest in experimenting with tropical fruits and vegetables. In such a case you could say something like this:

"Back at the office, when we talked about what you and Mrs. J. were looking for, you mentioned the importance of finding a home within easy access of your office. You also said that you did not want to be on a busy street and that you'd like some seclusion, too.

"Wouldn't you agree that this charming house does offer you just that? You'll be minutes away from your place of business, yet far enough away from the hustle and bustle noises of highway traffic. Being located in this wooded area also assures you of the peace and privacy you both want, doesn't it? And you'll have plenty of room on these spacious grounds to experiment with growing a variety of tropical fruits and vegetables. You'll both enjoy that, won't you?"

When you play back in such a manner what your prospect has told you, you act as a mirror reflecting feelings he previously revealed. In this way, you help him to form a clearer picture of his situation. It really helps him to comfortably arrive at the decision to buy or sell.

How to turn objections into reasons to buy

Whenever objections arise, some salespeople get panicky and respond with rebuttals. This generally annoys a prospect. However, it is wiser to first agree with him. Then, by repeating something he told you earlier, you can turn his objection into the very reason why he should go ahead now.

For example, the prospect may say, "The interest rates are too high. I think I'll wait until they come down."

You may answer him effectively as follows: "I understand how you feel. Right now the current interest rate of 12 percent does seem to be high. As you probably know, these rates fluctuate. Even though they may come down from time to time, the trend over the past several years has been steadily upward, hasn't it? And it does look like inflation will be with us for some time to come, wouldn't you agree?

"Sometime earlier you told me you were sorry you didn't buy last year when the rates were lower. That's why you wouldn't want to gamble now, would you, that the interest rates might possibly come down? Instead, you might find that they'll continue to climb even higher and, in the meantime, you are also taking a chance on losing this lovely home that has everything you and your wife want, isn't that so?

"You'll be interested to know that I figured the principal and interest at 12 percent, taxes, and insurance to be a total of about $580.00 per month. This is just about the amount that you said would be comfortable and easy for you to handle, isn't it?"

Using the summary technique

The summary technique is another excellent way to use feedback advantageously. Recently, at a seminar, I listened to a very successful Realtor discuss this technique, which he referred to as the "why letter." Since the time when he first learned of this method several years ago, he has made this "why letter" a standard procedure in his office. Every agent uses this letter after he has shown a property. It helps the prospect to make a favorable decision when he sees a list of why he should buy and why he should not. This is how it is done:

1. You, the salesperson, suggest that the prospects and you make a list of what they like and do not like about the property they are considering.
2. On a sheet of paper, draw an elongated "T."
   a. On the left side, write the heading, *PRO*
   b. On the right side, write the heading, *CON*
3. List all the favorable reasons for going ahead on the left side of the "T." (These are according to what they told you and agreed upon, and from their point of view.) Take your time so that you can make the list as long as possible. If you make it a joint venture, your prospects won't feel that they are being sold. They'll thoroughly enjoy participating and will probably contribute some important reason which you might have overlooked.
4. Then, continue listing, on the right side of the "T," the reasons why they shouldn't buy. These would include things they said they didn't like, things they questioned, or something you and they know is objectionable. Let the buyers come up with their own cons. They'll see that this side of the "why letter" will contain only a few items.
5. Get agreement on each item. As you record each of the reasons on your summary sheet, you'll want to make sure that your prospects understand and agree. They'll realize that these lists truly represent their thinking. By doing this, you are helping them to crystallize their thoughts and feelings. When they just glance at the completed summary, it will be obvious to them that the number of positive reasons for going ahead right now far outweigh the negative ones.

How an indecisive prospect was converted into a willing buyer

This case is a typical illustration of the successful use of the summary technique. You will see how feedback was used to overcome a prospect's hesitancy, to turn his objections into reasons for buying, and finally to help him arrive at the decision to purchase the home right then.

Young Don W. had just been discharged from the Navy. In two weeks he would start his new job as a nuclear engineer. He wanted a house near the power plant where he'd be working.

In the car, on our way to tour homes, I listened closely as Don and his wife, Marianne, chatted about their new life in Miami, how Don looked forward to playing golf and how much easier it would be to bring up their two-year-old son, Don, Jr., in year-round warm weather.

Of the two houses I showed them, they loved the second. Everything seemed to appeal to them—the location, the Mediterranean look, the patio for Donny to play in, the private yard, and the modern kitchen. They had no complaints.

As soon as we were ready to leave, buyer's fear began to set in. Don thought that perhaps they shouldn't rush into buying a house. He might want to use the money toward another car. Maybe they should rent for a while. After all, this was a new job. Maybe he'd be transferred or make a change in a year or two. He came up with quite a few excuses.

It was now noon. Little Donny was restless, it was hot, and everyone seemed weary. So I suggested having lunch. This would give us a chance to cool off, relax, and get some good food into our empty stomachs.

Toward the end of the meal, I decided it was time to use some feedback. I told Don and Marianne that I had been reviewing their situation in my mind and would like to share my thoughts with them. Then I began to recap the various things they had mentioned. It went something like this:

"You both like this house, don't you?"

"Oh, yes."

"You seemed delighted that there was a patio; you said it would be ideal for Donny to play in when he couldn't be outdoors in the yard. Isn't that so?"

"Yes."

"You mentioned that the location was perfect, the house being only minutes from work. Shopping is also convenient. These are important to you, aren't they?"

"Yes."

"As I understand, this is the price you had in mind, isn't it?"

"Yes."

"However, even though these requirements meet with your approval, I gather that you feel you should rent rather than buy because you are concerned about a possible transfer in a year or two. You also think you'd like to use the initial investment money to buy a car instead. These are your concerns at the moment, aren't they?"

"Yes."

"Well, Don, I think you can have your cake and eat it, too. As for the transfer, that should be no problem. You can sell your house in a year or two. You should be able to get your money out, in which case you will have lived there rent-free. Better still, if the real estate market continues as it has in the past several years, you should be able to make a profit as well. You wouldn't object to that, would you?"

"No, I'd like that."

"Don, I believe you can have your home *and* the money for the car. Let me tell you how. When we started out, you were talking about buying your home conventionally, which would, of course, mean a sizeable initial investment. You had not thought of using your VA eligibility, had you?"

"You're right. How would that work?"

"Fortunately, the house already has been VA approved. You have your Navy discharge papers, so now you can take advantage. You can buy the house on VA with nothing down. You'll have to pay only closing costs. You see, don't you, that you can have your house and still have the money to buy your car?"

"Yes, I see."

"In addition, you can save yourself the discomfort of driving Marianne and Donny around in the heat, looking for a place to rent, and getting more confused the more you look. By buying this house now, you can resolve your housing needs *and* you can enjoy the next two weeks playing golf. How would you like that?"

"That sounds great! You're right, I hadn't thought about using VA. I have to admit, this does seem to be a simple solution for us."

"Fine. Let's go back to the office and take care of the details."

As you can readily see, using feedback at the moment of indecision made closing easy.

Before leaving this example, I'd like to share with you a detailed analysis of the use of feedback in this sale.

I. Listening closely to the information divulged by Don and Marianne made it possible to advantageously play it back to them.

II. Summarizing, by repeating back what they had disclosed, produced "yes" answers. They agreed with the picture of their situation as it was presented.

III. Turning Don's objections into reasons to buy:
Objection—Rent for a while.
Solution—Buying now, they'd resolve their living situation, avoid the confusion and discomfort of looking further.
Objection—Use the down payment money to buy the car they needed.
Solution—Using Don's VA eligibility, there would be no down payment. They could have both the car and the house.
Objection—A possible transfer in a year or two. It may not be wise to get involved with owning a home at this time.
Solution—A transfer would not be likely to cause a loss, but might possibly end up providing a profit.

IV. Final summary of immediate benefits: Reminding them again that they could move right in, have the home they loved, the new car they said they wanted, *plus* an unexpected bonus for Don. He could have the joy of two weeks of golf.

Had I been able to put down the summary on paper, the summary sheet would have looked like this:

PRO	CON
like the house	maybe rent
Mediterranean look	possible transfer
appealing	use money to buy car
modern kitchen	
patio (for Donny)	
private yard	
close to work	
close to shopping	
right price	
VA eligibility	
house VA approved	
immediate occupancy	
two weeks of golf	

Using feedback to close easier, faster, and more often

Feedback is one of the most proven and powerful techniques used by successful real estate salespeople. Whether listing, showing, or negotiating, using feedback to clarify points in your clients' minds or to overcome their hesitations will help bring your transaction to a speedy, successful conclusion. Of all the communication and closing techniques available to you, feedback is the easiest to use and surest to succeed, because it allows the prospect to sell himself.

Checklist for Using Feedback Advantageously

Do you use feedback effectively by:

Turning objections, whenever you can, into reasons to buy now?

Reinforcing your prospect's own thoughts and feelings?

Using a summary sheet to close, and doing it with your prospect listing his reasons for and against?

Restating your prospect's responses to the property and getting agreement after each statement?

Reassuring your prospect of the right decision?

6

Not

Properly Qualifying

Your Real Estate Buyer and Seller

"The one big secret of success is to *find out what the other fellow wants, then help him find the best way to get it,*" claims Frank Bettger in his book, *How I Multiplied My Income and Happiness in Selling.*

This is particularly true in selling real estate. More sales are probably lost because a salesperson either neglects or is unable to find out exactly what the buyer needed or wanted, than for any other single reason. Let's take a look at some of the reasons why this happens:

- Perhaps you feel you have a "hot" buyer or seller. You're eager to get going quickly. In your haste, you have no time to get more details.

- You may not be "programmed" to think "prequalify." You try the trial and error method, meet with the prospect frequently, and get to know him a little better. You figure that you're bound to hit it eventually.

- Maybe you feel timid about inquiring into the personal matters of strangers. You're reluctant to invade another person's privacy.

- Perhaps you don't know what questions to ask or how to ask them.

Then again:

- Maybe you do know the right questions and how to ask them, but you're a bit too lazy and it takes too much time.
- You may be adept at getting the facts, but you neglect to hear or heed the motivating factors, what the prospect really wants—the very things that will make him take action to buy or sell.

THE BENEFITS YOU'LL GAIN

1. You'll be recognized by buyers, sellers, and those in the field as a professional, and they will want to do business with you.
2. Right from the beginning, you'll eliminate the "suspects" because you won't be wasting your time on the "maybes" or spinning your wheels needlessly. On the other hand, you'll be concentrating on the serious, bona fide prospects.
   a) You won't waste your time, energy, or money on sellers who only want to test the market, or on those who don't really care whether or not they sell their property.
   b) You won't waste your time on buyers who have been looking for a long time, the perpetual shoppers, or those who love to go looking at houses as a pastime.
   c) You'll direct your efforts toward working exclusively with people who are ready, willing, and able to perform.
3. You'll obtain complete and exact information. This will prevent you from going to the trouble of finding a property the buyer likes and getting the offer accepted by both buyer and seller, only to find that you can't consummate the sale because your buyer does not qualify for the mortgage loan.
4. You're not apt to hear that they bought something altogether different from someone else.
5. You'll be selling on purpose, not by accident. In other words, you won't be just an order taker. It won't be a case of showing them everything until they eventually say, "We like this one; we want to buy it," or waiting for some seller to say, "I'd like you to list my house."
6. Finally, as Mr. Bettger so aptly put it, "You'll master the one secret of success: you'll find out what people want, and help them get it."

TECHNIQUES YOU CAN USE TO GAIN THESE BENEFITS

Dispel the myth that "buyers are liars, sellers are too"

Now is the time to dispel the myth which we have heard all too often in the marketplace: "Buyers are liars, sellers are too!"

How many times have you heard a buyer say, "I want a three bedroom house," and then discovered that he bought a two or four bedroom house? Or a seller who says, "I won't take one penny less than $65,000," yet ends up selling for $61,500 or thereabouts? Did they lie? No, they compromised. They adjusted their thinking when it came time to make a final decision. At the time when they made the initial statements, they were being honest. That was how they felt, what they thought they wanted. When they realized that they could not get everything they wanted and needed, they compromised on some of the specifics, not on the emotional factors.

Surely, you have had the same experience when you have gone shopping for clothing, appliances, a car, or some other item. Think back. When you started out, didn't you have some preconceived notions about the color, style, or make, and then you ended up buying something totally different? Did you lie to yourself or to the salesperson? No, of course not. As you viewed what was available, you changed your mind; you compromised.

Emotion motivates

So it is with buyers and sellers of real estate. They are basically honest when they tell you initially what they want. At the time, that is what they thought they wanted. Although most people feel that they should be logical and practical in selling or selecting a house, they usually aren't. They really don't decide on the basis of their needs. Logic may persuade them, but emotions motivate them.

Many salespeople do not realize this. They take their customers and clients literally, and then end up angry and disappointed. For instance, they aren't aware that buyers may change their minds about specifics, such as number of bedrooms, price, or location. However, they will not change their minds so quickly about those things which they want most and which will provide them with emotional satisfaction. Here are a few typical emotional motivations—referred to as "hot buttons"—that turn real estate buyers on:

- Safe, quiet street for the children.
- Prestigious neighborhood.
- Traffic-free floor plan.
- Family room for entertaining.
- Trees and shrubbery.
- Minimum lawn care.
- Sewing room, workshop.
- Investment.
- Security.

These are the types of things people buy. They do not just buy a house. The house is incidental; it's thrown in. Think back on the sales you made recently and you'll spot the motivating factors in each case. Conversely, review some of the sales you lost and you'll probably discover that it was because you did not seek or heed the "hot buttons."

How one salesperson loses sales

While discussing this in class, a student and agent named Carmen testified that this was just what happened to her recently. Because of her friendship with the buyers, Carmen didn't qualify them in detail. She limited herself to following the specifics they gave her regarding area and price range. Much to her chagrin, she learned that her friends had bought a house in a completely different area, with different specifications, and in a different price range. Carmen recognized her mistake of not seeking the "hot buttons," and in the future she will be certain to be more thorough in qualifying all of her buyers.

Analyzing the problem first

When you go to a new doctor, you don't expect him to see you until you have answered a questionnaire about your medical history, covering from infancy to the present. No doctor would consider offering an opinion or prescribing a course of treatment until he was familiar with your medical records and had personally examined you. After this he would still want to discuss with you your feelings, aches, and pains. Sometimes, when he feels that the initial information is not adequate or conclusive, he recommends further studies, such as X-rays or blood tests. Finally, when he has sufficient information, he carefully considers all of the facts, at which time he makes his diagnosis and prescribes treatment.

An analogy between the doctor and the real estate agent demonstrates and emphasizes the importance of being thorough in analyzing the problem before offering the solution. The doctor solves a health problem; the agent solves a real estate problem, the enormously important problem of buying or selling property. It is probably the largest single investment decision anyone makes during a lifetime.

The doctor practices medicine, you practice real estate. Therefore, being a professional like the doctor, you should probe for facts and feelings by beginning with a questionnaire.

How to qualify with a questionnaire

Obviously, the reason for asking qualifying questions is to get information. In my real estate seminars, some of my most experienced students have told me that they were delighted and amazed at the advantages of using a prepared questionnaire. They hadn't realized what a difference it would make. They found it easy to employ, and they liked having a logical sequence to follow. But, most importantly, they could be certain that they wouldn't leave out any vital information. Previously, many of them had discovered after an interview that they had omitted some of the important items. Now they don't get sidetracked and don't have to trust to memory, because they can refer to a written record.

Handling inquiries

Generally, the initial inquiries regarding properties occur over the telephone. Not qualifying prospects on the initial call can waste a lot of time and can be totally unproductive. My experience has shown that the best results are gained when you determine, as quickly as possible, whether the caller is just a "suspect" to eliminate at once or a bona fide "prospect" worth pursuing further by making an appointment.

For this purpose, a brief prepared list of questions can be used effectively. I have developed such a list, called "A Buyer's Quickie Qualifying Questionnaire," which you can find on page 77. It has been quite successful for me, as well as for those who have attended my seminars. Like all of the handy forms presented in this book, this one can be used as is or changed to apply to your specific needs.

How to ask qualifying questions with the quickie questionnaire

When seeking information, some real estate agents sound like robots. They ask the questions automatically in a clipped, monotonous tone without any expression whatsoever. This is bound to have a negative effect on the other person. It makes the buyer or seller reluctant to answer questions, which, in actuality, are for his own benefit.

Here are a few tips to help establish good rapport from the start:

- Repeat the other person's name frequently. He loves to hear it, and it makes him more receptive.
- Speak in a friendly, conversational manner, as you would when talking to someone you know. He'll respond in kind.
- From your demeanor, let him know you care. You're not just curious—you really care.
- Do not add unnecessary comments, such as "good," "uh huh," or "O.K."
- Adjust your vocabulary and the speed of your conversation to that of the listener. It helps to establish good communication.
- Reword or rephrase any question that seems to cause confusion or misunderstanding.
- Start with opening remarks that will put the other person at ease, making him feel comfortable about giving you complete, confidential information.

For example: "Mrs. Buyer, in order for me to help you find just what you are looking for, in the price range you are interested in, there are some things I need to ask you. In that way, I'll know just what you have in mind and I'll be able to show you only those houses that I know you would like and that will meet your requirements. Then I know I won't waste your time by showing you the wrong houses. You'd like to be spared needless running around, wouldn't you?" As you can imagine, the usual response is, "Yes, indeed!"

A Buyer's Quickie Qualifying Questionnaire

Name_____Phone_____

Location preference_____

Price range considering_____No. bedrooms____No. baths____

Other rooms_____

Any other special requirements_____

Any additional particular preferences_____

How soon do you need a home?_____

Presently own or renting?_____If renting, lease expires_____

If own, do you need to sell your home first?_____

If sold, closing date_____

Where do you live now?_____

Any special plans for financing_____

Approx. amount considering as initial investment_____

Approx. amount considering as monthly investment_____

How many children?_____Ages_____

Wife or husband a veteran?_____

Have veteran's eligibility?_____

What does husband do?____Where?____For how long?_____

What does wife do?_____Where?_____For how long?_____

What is approx. combined yearly income?_____

How long have you been looking?_____

Have you seen anything you like?_____

Why didn't you buy it?_____

Anyone else involved in making a decision?_____

Are you working with any other real estate agent?_____

When will it be most convenient for you and your husband/wife
to look at some homes that will be chosen according to
specifications you have given me?_____

Morning_____Afternoon_____Day_____Other_____

Continue questioning in a friendly manner:

- "What price range are you considering, Mrs. Buyer?"
- "Mrs. Buyer, approximately how much cash do you expect to invest in your new home?"
- "And approximately what monthly investment did you have in mind?"
- "Are either you or Mr. Buyer veterans? Do you know if Mr. Buyer has his VA eligibility?"
- "Do you work, Mrs. Buyer? Where?"
- "What do you do, Mrs. Buyer?"
- "What kind of work does Mr. Buyer do? Where?"
- "To be certain we will be looking at the proper price range, may I ask for your total income, yours and Mr. Buyer's combined?"

After asking the questions, it is a good idea to verify and briefly summarize the salient points and once again ask if there are any additional particular preferences:

"Mrs. Buyer, I think I know what you have in mind, but I just want to make sure. From what you have told me, you want three or four bedrooms, two baths, preferably four, for about $60,000. You don't care much about a yard, but it is important for you to be on a quiet street, and the home must be close in so that you and your husband can get to and from work quickly and easily. You prefer a newer home, not over ten years old. Your home must have a two-car garage and a large family room. Is that right? Mrs. Buyer, I want to be sure to select homes that will be right for you, so please tell me if there are any other features you can think of that are important to you and your husband."

How to qualify a buyer's financial ability

Some salespeople have a mental block when it comes to asking for personal financial information. They feel shy about doing it or are afraid that the buyer might resent it. However, just as a patient expects a doctor to ask questions concerning his health, so does a buyer expect a real estate agent to question his financial ability to qualify for the mortgage. In fact, the buyer actually welcomes a professional approach to this matter because he is not always certain himself about just what he can afford.

An easy way to relax your buyer so that he'll realize that you are asking questions essentially for his own benefit and not just prying would be to say something like this:

> "Mrs. Buyer, to make sure we aren't wasting your time by looking at houses in the wrong price range, or being disappointed by finding a home you really love only to discover later on that you may not qualify at the present time for a mortgage, I need to ask you a few questions. You may be interested to know how we can arrive at a rough estimate by using what we call the rule of thumb method. The total price of your home should not exceed two and one-half times your gross yearly income, or put another way, your monthly investments should not exceed one week's salary. This is the guideline we can use now. May I ask, what is your approximate total income, that is, yours and your husband's combined salaries?"

Later on, when you need to get more accurate information, suggest something like: "In order to know exactly which home you can qualify for at this time, let's work out the details together." Then proceed to get complete, exact information about their income and outstanding debts so that you can arrive at the total price and monthly payments. If you don't have a form for this purpose, try using "4 Steps to Know Which Home You Can Afford," on page 80.*

How to learn more about buyer, seller, and property

You may recall in the first chapter that when Phoebe learned a little bit more about the property, it made a big difference in getting her low offer accepted. And in Chapter 4, my knowing that the N. children were adopted saved the sale so that Mr. and Mrs. N. could qualify for their mortgage.

There is still another case, a strange situation, which I'd like to share with you. It describes how one lister "flubbed" while another salesperson in his office sold one of *his* listings quickly to one of *his* prospects.

When an offer to purchase was being presented to the seller, John, the lister, was surprised when he noticed and recognized the

---

*Developed by and used by permission of AmeriFirst Federal Savings and Loan Association.

4 Steps to Know Which Home You Can Afford

Step 1 — Income

Summarize your monthly income. Include both your income and the income of your spouse or co-borrower. To calculate monthly income, multiply weekly wages by 4.33 and bi-weekly wages by 2.16.

INCOME SOURCES		GROSS MONTHLY INCOME
Salaries	you	
	co-borrower	
Commissions and Overtime (average of last 3 years)	you	
	co-borrower	
Dividends and Interest	you	
	co-borrower	
Other Continuing Income (Please specify)	you	
	co-borrower	
#1 TOTAL MONTHLY INCOME		

Step 2 — Debts

Include all regular payments made by you or your co-borrower for things such as loans, credit cards, etc. Do not include monthly payments that will be completed within the next seven months. Also, do **not** include utility payments.

DEBTS	UNPAID BALANCE	MONTHLY PAYMENT
Installment Debt (department store, Master Charge, etc.) (Please specify)		
Auto Loans		
Real Estate (Itemized)		
Other Debts (Itemized)		
Alimony and Child Support		
#2 TOTAL MONTHLY DEBT		

Step 3 — Home Payments

Using the table on the right, you will be able to estimate your monthly principal and interest payment on a 29-year loan at the current rate in effect. Remember, the mortgage amount does not include your down payment or closing costs.

HOME PAYMENTS	MONTHLY PAYMENT
Principal and Interest Payment	
1/12 of Annual Property Tax	
1/12 of Annual Property Insurance Premium	
Condominium Maintenance Fee	
#3 TOTAL HOME MONTHLY PAYMENT	

To Calculate Your Monthly Payment For Principal and Interest

Multiply the amount of your loan (in thousands) by the dollars per thousand in the table below.
Example for $35,000 loan at 10.25%:

$$\underset{\text{amount of loan}}{35} \times \underset{\text{dollars per thousand}}{9.01} = \underset{\substack{\text{monthly principal and} \\ \text{interest payment}}}{\$315.35}$$

Interest Rate	Monthly Payment Per $1000
10.00 %	$ 8.83
10.25 %	$ 9.01
10.50 %	$ 9.20
10.75 %	$ 9.38
11.00 %	$ 9.57
11.25 %	$ 9.76
11.50 %	$ 9.95
11.75 %	$ 10.14
12.00 %	$ 10.33

$$\underset{\text{amount of loan}}{\rule{2cm}{0.4pt}} \times \underset{\text{dollars per thousand}}{\rule{2cm}{0.4pt}} = \underset{\substack{\text{monthly principal and} \\ \text{interest payment}}}{\rule{2cm}{0.4pt}}$$

Step 4 — Pre-Qualify Yourself

You can now easily prequalify yourself on a specific home or determine the price range that is practical for your budget.

#3 Total Monthly Payment divided by $ _____ = _____ % (should be 28% or less)
#1 Total Monthly Income $ _____

#2 Total Monthly Debt divided by $ _____ = _____ % (should be 8% or less)
#1 Total Monthly Income $ _____

TOTAL _____ % (should be 36% or less)

---

*Developed by and used by permission of AmeriFirst Federal Savings and Loan Association.

names of the buyers, Mr. and Mrs. M. They were people to whom he had shown some of his other listings, but nothing had developed. Why had Maria, the other agent, sold them and he had not?

John had a number of townhouse listings in a particular neighborhood. In fact, townhouses were his specialty. When Mrs. M. called on one of his listings, he spent a few days showing Mr. and Mrs. M. some of his townhouses. None seemed to be right. Then, one day, Mrs. M. called the office in response to an ad. It was Maria's floor day, so she took the call. In qualifying, Maria learned that Mr. M. worked in a plant nursery. Immediately, Maria made arrangements to show Mr. and Mrs. M. one of John's listings. It was on a small lot, but it had a screened patio with about $4000 worth of beautiful plants. That did it! The M.'s bought the patio. The townhouse itself was practically incidental.

Making good use of extra information

Whatever extra information you do learn can be useful in convincing your prospect to buy a particular house. For example, you might influence your buyer by repeating some of the favorable feelings you know the seller has expressed, such as:

- "We like this house so well that we are duplicating the floor plan in the new home we are building. It's the same, identical house, just a larger version. If we didn't need the extra rooms, we would never consider moving."

- "We once considered putting in a pool, but we discovered how convenient it is for the children to walk to the lovely public pool. And they love swimming in an Olympic-size pool."

- "The children hate to leave, because they have many friends here."

- "If we weren't being transferred, we wouldn't dream of selling this house. It's perfect for us; this is a quiet, friendly neighborhood and we're close to shopping, too."

- "What I like about this house is having so much storage space. All of the closets are large. Where we are going, we won't have as many—I know I'll miss it."

Using information from the sellers

What you learn in advance about your seller can also be helpful in both listing and negotiating. For instance, it can be advantageous to know the following:

- How long has he lived there?
- Where is he going?
- Why is he selling? To take advantage of a profit? Because of divorce, transfer, death, or other personal matter? Because he wants a change of neighborhood, more grounds, larger or more expensive home?
- Does he have a date for moving?
- How long has his home been on the market?
- What results has he had so far? What offers?
- What kind of financing would he consider? VA? FHA? Conventional?
- Would he consider taking back a mortgage? Small or large?
- How did he arrive at the price he is asking?

Learn to walk in the other person's shoes

Up until now, we have discussed the importance of seeking the specific facts and emotional feelings of the buyer or seller. To complete this task successfully, you must empathize with them. That is, project your own personality into the personality of the buyer or seller in order to understand him better. Or, as the saying goes, "learn to walk in the other person's shoes."

This requires catering to the other person's ego, while at the same time submerging your own ego. However difficult it may be in the beginning, with practice you can train yourself. Here are some simple guidelines:

- Bear in mind that people don't care what you know until they know you care.
- Get off to a good start by saying, "I understand. I know how you feel." Continue with expressions such as, "From what you told me...," "You indicated that ...," "You mentioned that...," and then repeat their words or rephrase the statement, but always from their point of view.
- Avoid giving your opinions at all times. Don't decide for the other person. Remember that you are trying to see things through their eyes, so it doesn't matter what you think or feel. You have to divorce yourself completely from each situation.

A saleswoman I know nearly lost a sale because she was trying to show her prospects what she thought they ought to buy. The buyers, a young couple, had stated that they wanted a townhouse in a particular neighborhood. Jane, the agent, lined up a few townhouses but decided to drive them around and show them some private homes. She thought they ought to see what houses were available. Of course, they weren't at all interested in even looking at the houses. While riding around, they passed a "For Sale" sign in front of a townhouse complex. They wanted to see it. Jane reluctantly took them in and, much to her amazement, that is what they bought. Jane couldn't understand it. She would never want to live in such an undesirable neighborhood. Yet, none of the drawbacks she saw were deterrents for the couple. That was the townhouse they liked, wanted, and bought.

How to establish loyalty

You may work hard and conscientiously with a prospect and then lose him to another salesperson. It happens all too often. I think this happens simply because 1) you took them for granted, 2) you didn't train them to be loyal, 3) they didn't understand the workings of real estate, 4) they didn't know that Realtors cooperate, or 5) they didn't understand how Multiple Listings works. Regardless of which reason applies, it is your fault, not that of the buyers. Some people are under the impression that it is more beneficial for them to deal directly with the Realtor whose name is on a sign or in whose name the ad appears. They also don't understand that the price and commission are the same no matter which office sells it.

It's your job to educate them about what you want them to do. Therefore, in order to protect yourself and ensure their complete cooperation, you must educate your buyers in the very beginning and instruct them about what you want and expect them to do.

Explain to your buyers the benefits of working with you as their exclusive agent:

- You know exactly what they are looking for because you have carefully qualified them.
- You'll save them a great deal of time. You'll check out the details in advance so that they won't waste time and energy looking at properties or calling on ads that do not meet their needs. Those that are not right for them will be eliminated.
- Since Multiple Listing services provide you with whatever listings are available, you have exactly the same information as any other real estate salesperson. The buyers won't be duplicating their efforts by looking at houses they have already seen and know about.

- They will *not* save money on the commission if they deal directly with the office whose name appears in the ad or on the property sign. However, you will be in the best position as their representative to get the best price and terms for them. You will be able to do this because you know them, understand their circumstances, and are an expert in negotiating. (Explain briefly that the total commission fee is the same no matter who sells it. The fee, including the listing fee, is set by the seller when he signs his listing contract.)
- Of equal importance, and something most buyers do not think of at this time, is that after their offer to purchase has been accepted, you, as their agent, will follow through to make certain that the closing process will be as smooth as possible with a minimum amount of problems. The buyers are assured that you'll keep them informed at all times of the progress of the sale, so that they'll know what's happening.
- Add whatever other services you and your firm can offer to make buying a home a satisfactory experience for them.

Tell your buyers and remind them frequently what you expect of them:

- They should call you immediately if they hear about a house or see one that sparks their interest.
- They should call you immediately if they notice any appealing ads.
- They should call you immediately if they see an open house or "For Sale by Owners" that they may want to look at.

Explain your part in response to their calls: Assure them that you will carefully check out all of the information and make arrangements to accompany them to view only those houses that seem to meet their requirements.

Caution them: They should not, under any circumstances, attempt to view any homes on their own. Explain the real estate ruling that, as the selling agent, you must accompany your buyer on the initial viewing of the property. Further explain that this is the only way you are permitted to assist them.

Advance agreement

Before starting out, ask your customers if they are agreeable to following your instructions and willing to work with you exclusively as their agent to locate the right home for them. Otherwise, you may run the risk of wasting a lot of your valuable time with people who are not really promising prospects.

At the risk of sounding redundant, the following are some of the casual conversation openers you can use when asking your buyers to be loyal to you.

- "Mrs. Buyer, I'd like you to do me a favor. I want you to stay with me. If you see a sign or an ad by another broker, or hear of anything else that interests you, call me. I will do the checking and will get all of the information for you. I know exactly what you want. If any of the houses meet your requirements, I'll arrange to show them to you at your convenience."

- "If you happen to pass an "Open" sign on a house or read about it in the paper, don't be tempted to take a "look-see." Call me instead. I'll show it to you. Once you go inside without me, I can't help you even though you tell them you are working with me. Now that I know you and understand what you want, I'd like you to stay with me. I'd like to help you."

- "Mrs. Buyer, many people are not aware that the brokers in the area cooperate. That's the purpose of Multiple Listing—to share each other's listings. So, it doesn't make any difference which office sells the house. The price of the house and the commission the seller pays is the same for everyone, no matter who sells it. Therefore, there is absolutely no advantage whatsoever to you in dealing directly with the broker whose name is on the sign or in the ad."

You may have to keep repeating this to your prospects. They either won't understand, won't pay attention, or they will forget. Whatever the reason, you will have to keep reminding them each time you talk to them. "Have you seen any signs or ads that seem interesting to you? Tell me about them. I'll check them out and call you back."

In concluding this chapter, let me say that you now have the secret of successful salesmanship. If you follow these guidelines and use these techniques, you'll verify the validity of Mr. Bettger's wise advice: "The one big secret of success is to *find out what the other fellow wants, then help him find the best way to get it!*"

Checklist for Determining a Qualified Buyer and Seller

Do you prequalify your buyer by:

Using a "quickie" type questionnaire which provides personal information such as name, address, phone number, present living situation, employment, veteran eligibility, specific needs?

Asking about special features, the "hot buttons," that will turn the buyer on?

Asking day and time available to view properties?

Do you establish good rapport by:

Saying your client's name often?

Speaking in a friendly, conversational manner like when you talk to someone you know?

Not adding unnecessary comments?

Fitting your vocabulary and speed to your client?

Rewording any questions which confuse your client?

Do you financially qualify your buyer by:

Explaining and using the rule of thumb method?

Using the four-step method to get more specific information?

Do you make good use of "extra" information (favorable feelings your clients expressed)?

Do you use the following types of information for listing and negotiating:

How long has he lived there?

Where is he going?

Why selling?

• For profit, divorce, transfer, death, change of neighborhood, more grounds, larger or more expensive home, etc?

Date set for moving?

Length of time on market?

Results so far? Offers?

Financing he'd consider (VA, FHA, conventional)?

Willing to take back mortgage (small or large)?

How did he set price?

Do you show empathy by:

Showing you care?

Using phrases like, "I understand..." "I know how you feel..."?

Using phrases which restate what they said?

Avoiding giving your own opinion?

Do you establish buyer's loyalty by explaining the benefits of using you as their exclusive agent, by showing that you know exactly what they're looking for because:

You can screen carefully and thus save time?

You have access to the same information as any agent through Multiple Listing?

They won't save commission by dealing with the listing agent?

You will follow through and keep them informed?

You can offer the following additional services:

- Telling them frequently that you expect them to call about any houses of interest
- Appealing ads
- Open houses or "For Sale by Owners"?

Explaining consequences of viewing a home without you?

Getting advance agreement to call you for all houses of interest?

7

Failure to

Plan an Effective Listing Presentation

Mr. Reginald T., vice-president of a large international corporation, was being transferred to another part of the country. Before putting his charming home on the market, he visited some real estate offices in his area. He selected four firms that impressed him, interviewed one agent from each firm, and then chose the one he and Mrs. T. felt was best qualified to handle the listing on their home.

How did they decide which agent they wanted? Why did they choose Edna? What did she do or say that convinced them? Why had the other three failed?

The listing was a "cream puff," one that any salesperson would love to handle. It was beautiful, immaculate, spacious, a ten-year-old rancher with four bedrooms, two baths, and a large, attractive, screened pool and patio. The home was in a prime neighborhood, near the best schools. Of course, it was air-conditioned but, with weather permitting, the windows and sliding glass doors could be opened to the balmy breezes and the breathtaking view of the lush landscaping. All this plus a motivated seller made the listing a prime one.

Here's how Mr. and Mrs. T. came to their decision concerning Edna. According to Mrs. T., "Each of the four agents we interviewed seemed well-qualified, but we chose Edna because she seemed to be the most thorough in her preparation, particularly in presenting her comparative market analysis, which she explained in detail. She showed us what similar houses in the neighborhood sold for and when they were sold. In addition she told us all about the houses that were still on the market, how long they had been available and what prices the owners were asking. We appreciated this very much. It gave us a picture of the present market conditions and enabled us to arrive at a realistic price of $92,500, hopefully for a quick sale. All of this information was presented to us in a pleasant manner of sharing, rather than selling."

What about the other three salespeople? There was one other whom the T.'s had considered. She was familiar with both the builder and the model of their house. She appeared to know her field, but she wasn't prepared. To use Mrs. T.'s words, "She seemed to be winging it." The third agent gave the T.'s the impression that she was more interested in the buyer than in the seller. The fourth rambled on and didn't seem to be familiar with either the property or the area. They didn't have much confidence in him and he surely was no help in determining the price since his suggestion was too high.

It seems evident that Edna was chosen as their agent because she had a well-prepared presentation geared to telling the T.'s what they wanted to know and hear.

Listing is the name of the game, but not many know how to play

In the real estate business there is a truism: "If you can't list, you can't last." Listings are the merchandise on our shelves. In other words, they are our stock in trade. Without them, a real estate firm cannot survive in business. Because listing is so vital to the success of every real estate salesperson, and because it generally takes two visits to be both professional and effective, I have devoted two chapters to this purpose. This chapter, on the mistake of not planning, covers how you can effectively gather information when you inspect the house. The next chapter will deal with the mistake of not executing an effective listing presentation when you bring back your recommendations and are face-to-face with the owners.

THE BENEFITS YOU'LL GAIN

1. You'll be efficient, thorough, and well-organized.
2. You'll have more control of your time. You will be able to schedule your listing appointments to your convenience.
3. You'll be confident and more convincing.
4. You'll have definite guidelines to follow. You won't have to trust your memory.
5. You won't omit or overlook essential details. You'll collect complete information.
6. You'll familiarize yourself with helpful particulars concerning both the property and the owners.
7. You'll have time to study and review the information before making recommendations.
8. You'll personalize your presentation based on the specific information you assemble.
9. You'll win the owners' trust and confidence. They'll be impressed by your professional approach.
10. The owners will accept more readily your carefully prepared recommendations for price, terms, and benefits related to your listing service.
11. And, of course, you'll have a much better chance of obtaining saleable listings.

TECHNIQUES YOU CAN USE TO GAIN THESE BENEFITS

Have a planned, not canned, presentation

Should you have a prepared presentation? And if you do, won't it sound stereotyped? Won't it turn homeowners off? Yes, you should have a prepared presentation, but no, it does not have to sound stereotyped.

Successful listers do have well-prepared, planned presentations. Even though the presentation is planned, it is not necessarily "canned." The basic ideas as well as the key words and phrases stay the same, but changes are made to adapt to particular prospects and selling situations.

While developing a prepared presentation, it is also important for an effective sales story to include committing questions in order to obtain commitments as you go along (see Chapter 3).

Once you have developed and practiced your prepared presentation, it will sound very natural, personalized, and convincing. Even though a fine actor repeats the same lines night after night on stage, he makes you feel that he *is* the very character he is portraying, that he is not simply reading his lines. So it is with the lines you recite at your listing appointments. These begin when you view the property.

Getting to know the property and the homeowner

Even though you may be familiar with the model, it is to your advantage to politely request a tour of the home. It not only makes the homeowners feel important, but it also gives you an opportunity to become acquainted with them as well as with the house.

As you proceed slowly, if you encourage the owners, they'll point out the features they feel are important for you to know and the features they particularly enjoy. This slow tour is an ideal time to break the ice, an easy way to relax them so that they can begin to look upon you as a friend, not a fearful foe.

You can achieve this by casually making brief, favorable comments about what you observe, interspersed with questions: "What a delightful view! How do you feel about leaving all this? Who is the artist in your family? What an interesting wall treatment! Are you planning to leave these wall brackets? What about the dining room chandelier, will it remain with the house?"

Whatever you learn, make a mental note and include it later with your data information, so that it can be beneficial when you make your presentation.

Here are some questions to ask, either during the tour or when you take down the specific data information:

- "Why are you selling?"
- "Do you have a time limit?"
- "Where are you going?"
- "How long has your home been on the market?"
- "What results have you been getting from your ads?"
- "Have you had any offers to date?"
- "Approximately how long do you want to try to sell on your own before considering professional help?"

This information may indicate a lack of motivation on the part of the sellers, in which case you'll want to eliminate them altogether.

Inspecting the property

When inspecting a home, some salespeople make the mistake of getting involved in or sidetracked by irrelevant discussions. Some even make negative remarks about the property or offer unwelcome suggestions for improvements. This wastes time, often annoys the owner, and gets the agent off to a bad start.

You can avoid this situation if you follow a routine procedure, and that is to limit your conversation to making favorable but brief comments, combined with asking pertinent questions. Even though the lady of the house may be directing the order of the showing, it is you who must maintain control of the conversation in order to be effective.

After the tour you might suggest: "Mrs. Owner, may we sit at a table so that I can record all the specifics of your house?"

Recording the specifics

In order to obtain complete information, you'll want to use some prepared form that covers the essential information about the homes in your area. On page 94, you will find a sample "Inspection Information Form."

You will put the owner at ease if you ask the questions in a pleasant, conversational manner: "Mrs. Owner, there are four bedrooms and two baths, isn't that right? And the address is 1234 Main Street? Do you happen to have the legal description of your house handy? At the same time, could you locate your tax and mortgage records?" (If not, assure her that you can get them yourself.)

Continue with the questioning. Follow the order on your prepared sheet, with the exception of filling in the price. Leave the price until last. Read aloud and check each item, even if you know it doesn't apply: "You do have a screened porch. There is no pool." Continue casually: "Mrs. Owner, to whom do you pay your mortgage? What is your first name, and your husband's?" Write down under *Remarks* whatever additional information is volunteered. If more room is needed, use the reverse side. Homeowners appreciate and are impressed by thoroughness. It indicates interest and competency.

Leaving the price until last

After all the information is filled out, ask about the price: "Mrs. Owner, what price have you been asking for your home?"

INSPECTION INFORMATION FORM

Date_____ _____ U. ____ Beds _____
                           Price: _____ F. ____ Baths _____

Address:_____

Size of lot:_____Zoning:_____

Legal: _____

Folio No. _____

Schools _____

Type const._____Roof:_____Floors:_____Blt:_____
_____ No. Stories   _____ Pool   _____ Water Heater
_____ Living Room   _____ Fireplace   _____ Water
_____ Dining Room   _____ Bedrooms   _____ Sewer
_____ Kitchen   _____ Baths   _____ Sprinkler
_____ Refrigerator   _____ Den   _____ Condition
_____ Stove   _____ Family Room   _____ Vacant
_____ Dishwasher   _____ Windows   _____ Possession
_____ Disposal   _____ Heat/Air-Cond. _____ Awn.-Shutters
_____ Screened Porch   _____ Garage or C/P _____ Sign O.K.

Remarks: _____
_____
_____

Taxes: City:_____ Homestead Exempt:_____
            County:_____ Insurance:_____

Terms:_____

Mortgage Loan #

1st Mtg._____ Amt:_____ _____% Int.___/mo PI_____
2nd Mtg._____ Amt:_____ _____% Int.___/mo PI_____
Commit._____ Amt:_____ _____% Int.___/mo PI_____

Owner:_____Date Listed_____
Address:_____Exclusive_____
Phone:_____To Show:_____Listed By_____

Address	Br/Bth	Stories	Blt.	Price

Subject to omissions, errors, and prior sale without notice.

She might say, "But that is without a real estate commission," or, "We are asking the same amount with or without a salesman. We are quoting one price to everyone." Make no comment other than, "I understand." You might add, "I'd be interested to know how you and Mr. Owner arrived at your price." If she asks, "What do you think about the price?" you may respond, "Now that I have seen your house, I'd like to review all the information and do some research before giving you a definite answer. When would be the best time for you and your husband to get this information and other information that will, I think, be helpful? Tomorrow at 7:00 or 7:30? Which is more convenient?"

How to handle "We still want to try to sell it ourselves"

If Mrs. Owner seems motivated, yet still insists that she and her husband are going to sell by themselves, you should then say, "Mrs. Owner, I know how you feel. I can understand that you would like to save the commission fee if possible. I don't really blame you for trying. May I ask approximately how long you and your husband plan to try on your own before considering professional help?" Whatever she answers, say, "Well, then, this is the best time to explain to you both how I can get you the highest price for your home, as quickly as possible and with the fewest problems. That is really what you want, isn't it? Well, that's what I'd like to explain to you and Mr. Owner, so if and when you are ready for professional assistance, you'll know whether or not you would like to employ me as your agent. Is tomorrow evening or Saturday noon more convenient?"

This kind of approach implies that all you want is an opportunity to explain your service. Since there is no feeling of obligation to list now, the homeowner generally feels secure in granting the appointment. With this appointment made, you can now make the final preparations for your listing appointment.

Personalizing the presentation

You promised that when you returned you would give the sellers a fair market price for them to ask, and at the same time you would explain what services you could offer them if and when they'd decide to seek professional help.

To show the homeowners how you arrived at the price for their home, you'll find it convenient and convincing to use a

COMPARATIVE MARKET ANALYSIS

Prepared for _____ Date _____

Subject Property

Suburb _____

Address	Br/Bth	Features	Adj. Sq. Ft.	Assess Value	Lot Size	Yr Blt

Current Listings

Address	Br/Bth	Features	Adj. Sq. Ft.	Assess Value	Lot Size	Yr Blt	Date List	Price List

Sold Properties

Address	Br/Bth	Features	Sq. Ft.	Assess Value	Lot Size	Yr Blt	Date List	Price Sold	Date Sold

Suggested price _____

As of this date _____

Agent _____

prepared form. People do believe and understand more easily what they see in print. If you don't already have a form for this purpose, the "Comparative Market Analysis" on page 96, is a sample of one that is easy to explain to sellers.

To effectively explain the services you offer, what you do and how, you'll want to assemble as much pertinent material as possible. In addition to the exclusive right of sale forms, these would include such items as brochures of similar properties that sold quickly, testimonial letters, or whatever else you might need to be convincing. Once you have designed your presentation to fit this particular property and its owners, you're ready to move into the next phase—executing the listing presentation.

Checklist for Planning an Effective Listing Presentation

Do you prepare to get your listing by:

> Getting to know the property and the owner, and getting a tour by the owner?

> Making brief favorable comments to draw out the owner's feelings and get information?

> Asking the following:
> Why selling?
> Time limit?
> Where going?
> How long on the market?
> Results?
> Offers to date?
> How long before willing to give to agent?

> Avoiding irrelevant discussion, making suggestions for improvements, etc.?

> Completing a prepared inspection form?

> Using a relaxed manner?

> Leaving price until last?

Do you request time to review or schedule to discuss price, services, and then prepare comparative market information?

> Assemble exclusive right of sale forms, similar property brochures, testimonials, etc.?

Do you feel confident about doing the best job for the seller?

8

Failure to

Execute an Effective

Listing Presentation

The great listing secret

Listing a house and selling a house are very similar. The big difference, however, is not in *how* you sell, but in *what* you sell. When you deal with a buyer, you are selling a particular *product,* something you can see, something tangible. When you deal with a seller, you are selling a *service.* That is different because it is intangible. Despite the difference, the competent real estate agent uses the same salesmanship techniques in talking to a seller and in determining the wants and needs of a buyer (see Chapter 6). He knows that in both situations the same secret of successful salesmanship applies: "Find out what the other fellow wants, then help him find the best way to get it."

Let's elaborate a bit further on this tested and proven strategy. First, let us clarify the words *the other fellow.* When listing, the other fellow is, of course, the homeowner, the seller. Now the question is, "What is it that the seller wants most?" Primarily, a seller wants to be assured and convinced of three things. These three things provide the key to the *Magic Listing Secret.* They are:

1. You will get the highest price for the sale of his home.
2. You will sell his home as quickly as possible.
3. You will do it with a minimum of problems.

These are the major concerns of every homeowner. Once he believes you can do these three things for him, he'll hire you as his agent to sell his house.

Before directing your efforts toward convincing the seller that you can satisfy these wants for him, let's try to understand his thinking.

Understanding the seller's thinking

First, getting the highest price for the sale of the home is without a doubt the most important item for all sellers. That happens to be the main reason why any owner tries to sell his home himself. He thinks he will save the commission fee and end up with more money in his pocket.

Second, selling the home quickly is also a great concern to the owner. He's fearful that he may not get the action he desires and needs. When he is considering a Realtor, he feels he ought to test the service to see if they'll actually deliver what they promise. Therefore, to protect himself, he either offers an open listing, or he opts for a short listing period. In his own words, "I don't want to be tied up for six months."

Third, encountering the fewest number of problems is still another important consideration for the seller. He wants to feel certain that he and his family will be relieved of the responsibilities and worries of selling his home. He'd like to feel confident that it will be an easy transition for them.

THE BENEFITS YOU'LL GAIN

1. Sellers will be more cooperative. They'll truly understand and appreciate what you do, how you perform, and how you can help them sell their home.
2. When you have listings, you control the market. You will automatically attract buyers for your listings and also for your other properties.
3. You'll have other sales associates working for you. They'll help to sell your listings.

4. Listings will give you continuous exposure. Signs on the properties and your ads will generate more listings and sales for you.

5. Sellers will be tied to you by contract, whereas buyers will not.

6. You'll build a solid referral business for your continued success.

7. Best of all, with exclusive listings, you'll be protected and paid well no matter who sells them.

TECHNIQUES YOU CAN USE TO GAIN THESE BENEFITS

Sell the service, not statistics

Once a salesperson understands what a homeowner really wants, he or she can then show the seller the best way to get what he wants. This does not mean dwelling on statistics, such as how many agents are in your office or how many listings your office has. What the seller does want to know is, "What's in it for me?" His prime interest is to find out how all this will personally affect him. He's only interested in knowing how you and your office perform, what the results are of the service you are offering. In other words, why should he hire you?

You should personalize your presentation and design it to include in detail the benefits to him for using the services of 1) a Realtor, 2) your company, and 3) you as his exclusive agent. For this purpose, try following this formula: *Perceive, Promise, Prove, Persuade.*

Perceive the problem

It isn't enough for you to be aware of what your seller wants; you must also share this awareness with him. Point out his problems to him. Let him know you understand. Get him to agree and confirm that what you have told him is what he wants most. For the benefit of emphasis, repeat and remind him frequently during your presentation: "Mr. Seller, what you want is to get the highest price for your home, have it sold as quickly as possible and with the absolute minimum of problems, isn't that so?" He will have to agree that this is what he wants.

Promise the solution

To assure the homeowner that you have the marketing tools and the know-how to successfully sell his home, review with him your prepared list of the numerous advantages you and your firm will provide for him. The emphasis should be on the special benefits your firm offers, in addition to the various things you do personally that make you both unique and capable of solving his problems. Too often, a salesperson assumes that the other person not only fully understands, but also appreciates what is being offered. For full impact, it is important to embellish on each item.

"Mr. and Mrs. Homeowner, as your agent there are many things I can do for you that will produce the results you want.

"First, we can give you maximum exposure to attract many buyers. Mr. Right Buyer might come to us from one of many sources:

- "He may come through our Multiple Listing Service. As you may know, over 2000 salespeople will be immediately alerted. They will be put on notice that your home is being offered for sale. These salespeople, too, will go to work for you. That's instant selling power, wouldn't you agree?"
- "He may be one of our present prospects. We continuously receive calls from prospective buyers because we are in the business."
- "He might drop in on one of our open houses."
- "He might answer one of the many ads we are currently running in the newspapers and magazines."
- "Or he might call on one of our many For Sale signs."

"Do you see, Mr. and Mrs. Homeowner? You can have the advantages of mass marketing, have instant selling power, and expose your home to a great many qualified buyers.

"Second, we can sort out prospects. There are three kinds of people who look at houses:

- "The first kind is in a hurry to move. They almost always go to a real estate firm because they know that the real estate agent can show them the most homes in the price range and type that they want."
- "The second kind has no urgency to move. They are usually looking for a real bargain. Their plan is to avoid the real estate commission fee and they usually do. For this reason, as a general rule, houses are sold by owners for 9½ percent less than homes sold through a real estate agency."
- "The third kind is just looking at houses because they like to. They can't afford to move or really don't want to. They always go to the owners directly because they are not serious."

"Can you see, Mr. Homeowner, how I can spare you from having the bargain hunters, the speculators, and the unqualified lookers coming through your home?

"*Third,* I can help you determine the right price, that is, the fair market value. Surprising as it might seem, people who sell their homes often set the prices much lower than necessary. Usually, however, the price is set too high, and the home does not sell. It takes a lot of work on our part, but we can help you select the best price to ask.

"Can you see how important it is and how we can help you to select the right market price?

"*Fourth,* I can sell prospects on taking action. Even a good prospect becomes fearful and needs urging to make a commitment. If he is looking at several homes, I'm in a better position to help him decide on this home.

"Do you see how selling experience can help you get a quick sale?

"*Fifth,* we are available 24 hours a day, seven days a week. Your property is never off the market.

"Do you see how we don't miss out on any opportunity for a possible buyer?

"*Sixth,* we can bargain better. When a buyer makes an offer directly to the owner, the owner cannot negotiate. As a third party, we are in a much better position to help maintain the asking price, without losing a serious buyer. Most often, the difference right here is more than the commission involved.

"Do you see how we are in the best position to get the most money possible and not lose a qualified buyer?

"*Seventh,* as your agent, when the right buyer is found, I will obtain a satisfactory deposit, sign the buyer to a legally correct purchase order, arrange escrow, and through my many contacts help obtain satisfactory financing. I'm good at getting signed contracts. I sell a large percentage of my own listings myself.

"Can you see how we can help to make the sale secure?

"*Eighth,* we can cut through a lot of red tape. Once an offer is accepted by you, there is an enormous amount of paperwork to be done. Since we live with this every day, we know the shortcuts necessary to process the mortgage and abstracting work and a multitude of other details.

"Can you see how we can save you, Mr. Homeowner, a lot of work, problems, and running around?"

Continue enumerating the promises of what you will do personally. For instance:

- Carefully verify and submit complete information on the home.
- Be creative in developing the most effective remarks in the brochure and ads.
- Call in advance to clear appointments for showing and holding open house.
- Stress complete cooperation with other agents who show the home.
- Report regularly on activity and, what is equally important, lack of activity.
- Promptly bring and explain all offers.
- After a contract is accepted, check constantly with all parties involved in the sale—selling agent, sellers' attorney, buyers' attorney, and mortgage company. Keep your buyer and you, the seller, informed of the progress of the sale.
- Offer assistance whenever it can be helpful.
- Add whatever else you or your company offers toward finalizing a satisfactory sale.

How to prove it

Along with the promises, present proof that you do deliver. Most homeowners want to be shown, and rightly so, that you can and will do what you promise. You should show as you tell. It is a known fact that people believe and remember more of what they see than of what they hear. When you furnish printed evidence to prove your point, the facts become credible and persuasive.

Ways to tell and show

First and foremost, show some proof of your statements. Do so as you are explaining them to the homeowner. Here are a few examples:

- Tell the homeowner that you are creative in developing effective remarks in your brochures and ads. Show your most productive work. For contrast, show some samples of wording which would fail to induce or invite a sale.
- Tell the owner that you get complete and accurate information. To demonstrate this, show your Multiple Listing brochures. Explain the dangers and problems that arise when mortgage information is incorrect or when items are incorrectly listed.

- Tell the homeowner that you and your firm have a good record of selling properties quickly. Show some Multiple Listing brochures on homes that you or your firm sold quickly. Write across them boldly, and in large letters written with a red magic marker, "Sold in 14 Days," "Sold in 5 Weeks," "Sold in 20 Days." Call their attention especially to those listings that are appropriate because of similarity in price and location, thus demonstrating your point.

- Tell the seller that you will help him arrive at a fair market price for his home. Show the form you use. Explain it slowly and simply. Explain how and why you arrived at the price you recommended for his consideration.

Use testimonial letters for powerful influence

Over the years, successful insurance agents have been using testimonial letters from satisfied customers to influence prospects. Selling life insurance is considered one of the most difficult kinds of selling, much like listing real estate, in that it involves selling an intangible, a service. Insurance men have discovered the powerful influence such letters can have on their prospects. I, too, have found this to be true. I have realized the benefits of collecting and using letters from satisfied buyers and satisfied sellers.

Keep them in reserve for a time when you may have a prospect who seems to like you, yet is hesitant and appears apprehensive. You still are a stranger to him. He needs to be reassured. Now is the time to effectively introduce this third party influence, your testimonial letters. At this point, show him one or two appropriate letters along with the corresponding listing. This is guaranteed to impress and you will no doubt witness a changed attitude in your prospect. This is just what was needed. These letters sell silently. They say, "Don't take my word for what I am telling you; here is what someone else, another homeowner like yourself, has said." The prospect can identify with the writer of these letters.

Persuade

So far, we have discussed the first three parts of the formula for solving the seller's problems. You captured his attention and helped him *perceive* his problem by crystallizing his thoughts about what he wants most. Then you *promised* him solutions to his problems, followed by *proof* that you can and will do what you promised. Now, all that is left to do is to *persuade* him to hire you as his agent. Since you no doubt incorporated in your presentation the various techniques covered in the first five chapters, it should be part of the normal course of events to ask for and obtain the sellers' signatures on the listing agreement. As in all closing situations, many agents are timid about asking for the order. You won't be when you realize that the owners expect you to ask them, and they would be disappointed if you didn't.

Keeping the door open

No matter how good the presentation is, a salesperson should realize that all sellers can't be sold the first time, and every listing is not worth pursuing. However, if you feel that it is a saleable listing and the sellers are motivated, be sure to keep the door open for return visits. Before leaving, politely thank the owners for their time and the privilege of inspecting their home. Then, conclude with the promise to return: "Mr. and Mrs. Homeowner, thank you very much for the privilege of inspecting your home and for the opportunity to meet you and explain what we can do to help you sell your home. I understand that you would like to continue trying to sell it yourself before considering professional help. In the interim, I'd like very much to keep in touch with you. I'll bring you any new information that I think might be helpful to you. If any questions should arise concerning financing, writing a contract, or anything else, please call me for the answers. You have my card, so don't hesitate to call. I'll be glad to help you, without any obligation, of course."

The return visit

Although you will plan your return visits for a time when you expect both husband and wife to be at home, the drop-in should appear to be casual rather than deliberate. Otherwise, they may resent it. Explain that you are on your way to or from some business. It could be an open house, a preview for a prospective buyer, or maybe you were just passing by. Be truthful at all times; there is never a reason to be dishonest.

Tell them that you wanted to share the new information you brought. This could be anything new or different, such as changes in the mortgage market, houses in the neighborhood that were sold recently or came on the market, special articles, forms, or anything you think might be of interest to them. Also tell them that you have been thinking about them, wondering how they were getting along, what results they have been getting from their ads, and if they have encountered any problems so far. This is a great time to let them talk freely. They'll probably reveal their thinking and their feelings, whether they are encouraged or getting discouraged with the activity to date. What they say can be the very reasons why they should hire you. You can use these valuable clues to close now and be on your way to building up your inventory of good, saleable listings.

How to ensure your commission

Some real estate agents do not hesitate to work on open listings. Although at times you may be tempted, especially when the transaction involves huge sums of money, don't do it. Whenever you show property without protecting your commission, you are always working from a position of weakness. Open listings can cost you thousands and thousands of dollars in lost commissions.

To make sure you get paid, you can tailor a written agreement to cover various and specific conditions, including a time limit. In some situations, only a day or two is all you need before submitting the offer. And when you do, you'll be surprised to find that the seller will usually cooperate. Whatever the circumstance, you'll always ensure your commission when you ask for and secure some sort of written listing agreement.

It had to be a two-week listing

It was Christmas-time, when most real estate salespeople feel it's a waste of time to be working; once everyone is out shopping, no one is going to be looking at houses. Nobody had told me this, so I was enthusiastically calling on "For Sale by Owner" homes. I was a novice and didn't know any better. Mrs. H. welcomed my call. Fortunately, when I arrived her husband was also home. I was in luck. It was easier to talk to both of them at the same time than to talk to Mrs. H. first and try to get back to see her husband later.

Their house was sparkling and well cared for inside and out. In addition, the location was tops. It was one of the most sought after areas for young families, where country club living was at its best. And the price was right. Who could ask for more?

After inspecting the property, Mr. H. told me his tale of woe. They had put a deposit on a house they dearly loved. The builder had taken the deposit with one condition. He'd hold the house for them until the first of January. They would have to produce a contract on their existing home on or before that date, or else he'd return their deposit.

It was now two weeks before the deadline and the H.'s had no contract. Mr. H. was frustrated and didn't know what to do. He would welcome the help of a Realtor, but all he had was two weeks time.

I told the H.'s that I had an idea. It was an unusual idea, something I had never tried before. I didn't know if it would work, but if they were willing, I certainly would give it a try: "How about a two-week exclusive right of sale listing?" Of course, I couldn't put it on Multiple Listing, but I could advertise it, hold it open nearly every day, put our sign out front, and contact and notify other agents. I'd really try hard to get them a contract within the allotted time of two weeks. Out of desperation, Mr. and Mrs. H. accepted the idea without hesitating.

Their house did sell within the first week. One day, another salesman was out showing houses to a couple of young newlyweds.

They were delighted when they spotted the "Open" sign.

Once they saw the inside, they couldn't resist buying it. Everyone was happy, but no one more than the H.'s. They couldn't believe it could happen. I hadn't been sure either, but the $900 commission convinced me that it was definitely worth the try.

Points to ponder

- Take advantage of the golden hours of evenings and weekends.
- Tap the ready market of referrals, FSBOs (For Sale by Owner), and expired listings.
- Husbands generally have the final say in selling a home.
- Respect the owners' feelings about selling the home themselves.
- Sellers are impressed by professionalism, enthusiasm, honesty, sincerity, promptness, and courtesy.

Finally, remember that a listing is a liability until it is sold. Then it becomes an asset. In this chapter, you have learned the importance of procuring listings as the first step in the success of a real estate sales career. We have explored the benefits and techniques for developing an effective listing presentation. Most agents recognize the importance of acquiring good, saleable listings, but many do not fully reap the rewards. They neglect to properly service their listings. **That is the next mistake real estate salespeople make, and you will read about it in Chapter 9.**

Checklist for Executing an Effective Listing Presentation

Do you try to follow the secret for successful listing?
>Adapt your presentation to fit the seller's situation and his attitude?
>Refrain from introducing impersonal statistics?
>Include special benefits to him for employing you and your company?

Do you convince the seller that you could satisfy his three basic needs of getting the highest price, in the shortest time, with the fewest problems?
>Explain what you would do?
>Provide widespread marketing exposure for the home?
>Sort prospects and save your client time and hassle?
>Help determine the best selling point?
>Help get a quick sale?
>Make yourself available 24 hours a day?
>Bargain better?
>Get a satisfactory deposit?
>Cut through red tape?
>Reinforce your promises with some positive evidence?

Do you find an excuse for a return visit?

Do you make the most of the call-back?
>Time it well?
>Spark and revive the owner's interest with something of particular interest and benefit to him?
>Encourage him to reveal and review his situation to date?

Do you have the attitude that you will get the exclusive right of sale listing?

9

Failure to

Effectively Service the Listing

"What seems to be the trouble?" Mr. L. wanted to know. "Our house has been shown daily. Many people have looked at it. Yet we haven't received a single offer. I just don't understand. What do you think is wrong? Is it the price?"

Before answering, I asked Mr. and Mrs. L. if they would think back to the original interview: "Do you recall that I mentioned at that time that part of our service was to offer suggestions that would help to make your home more saleable and appealing to potential buyers? I explained that, from our experience, we know that buyers don't usually have much imagination. They seem to appreciate only what they see. Therefore, they tend to overlook the full potential that a house has to offer. In view of this, I recommended painting the inside of your house in a very light color, perhaps an off-white, at the same time removing a few of the paintings from the walls. This would make the rooms appear larger and much brighter. I pointed out that, as it is now, even though the rooms are unusually spacious, they seem half their size because of the dark walls and the number of paintings. The combination of the dark walls on the inside and the hurricane shutters on the outside does cut down considerably on the light.

"You do remember, don't you, that when we discussed this, you objected to doing any painting? You said that you didn't think it was necessary and you felt that whoever bought the house would prefer to choose their own colors anyway.

"Well, I too have been concerned about the lack of offers in spite of all the activity. So, to make doubly sure about what I suspected, I checked with several of the salespeople who have shown your house. It may surprise you to know that none of them felt that the price was too high. In fact, the consensus was that your home is priced right, and that it is a nice house, in a most desirable neighborhood. The major complaint has been that the house is too dark. They say that their buyers prefer and are buying homes in the area that are bright and airy looking."

That did it. The L.'s admitted that they had previously been very reluctant to do any painting, but now they agreed to do it. In fact, Mrs. L. volunteered to do it herself.

Sure enough, within two weeks I sold the house to a very nice young attorney and his teacher wife as their first home.

You may think that suggesting that the seller paint the walls a light color is insignificant, but it was an important part of the service I had promised and rendered to the L.'s. Reporting back regularly and letting them know the reaction of prospective buyers confirmed the need for them to spruce up the appearance of the house in order to invite offers. This service actually converted the L.'s from suspicious and skeptical sellers to very cooperative clients, especially during the negotiating period. It was this kind of service that helped to make the $60,000 sale possible within the first five weeks of the listing.

How to avoid a seller's most common complaint

Since listings are your basic stock in trade, once you've procured them you'll want to make the most of each and every one. The best way to do this is by properly servicing them. This means giving your client continuous special assistance and advice to help him sell his property as quickly as possible. This service is a responsibility you assume the moment your seller signs the listing agreement, and it continues through the final closing. It is unfortunate but true that too many real estate agents make the mistake of shirking this responsibility. This is evidenced by marketing studies which indicate that the biggest complaint about real estate salespeople is that a seller may have signed a contract and not seen a salesperson since.

You may have run into this attitude when you have been out seeking listings. All too often sellers say, "I don't want to have anything to do with a real estate salesman. John Jones of XYZ Company insisted that he could sell our house quickly. He promised all kinds of things and was very persistent up until the day we signed the listing agreement. But ever since then, we haven't seen hide nor hair of him. We have no idea what's going on. We would never go through this again." A seller may also complain, "You real estate salesmen are all alike. You make all kinds of promises ahead of time, but after you get the listing you don't care!"

A grievance like this is damaging to your reputation and does indeed create a poor image of the real estate profession. To prevent this, you must effectively service every listing.

THE BENEFITS YOU'LL GAIN

1. You'll establish good rapport with your employer, the seller. He'll know that you understand him and the property. He'll realize that you are primarily concerned about him and his problem.

2. It'll help to remove resistance and, especially when it comes time for a price adjustment, your seller will be receptive.

3. Your seller will have trust and confidence in your ability. He'll see you deliver what you promised.

4. Your seller will become a partner. He'll consider the selling of his home a joint venture.

5. It will be easier to negotiate the offer to purchase. Chances are, your seller will even help you work out the acceptable price and/or terms.

6. You'll prevent possible problems at closings, or losing the sale altogether. When you present accurate and complete information, you'll avoid serious errors and omissions.

7. Other associates will cooperate. They'll help to sell your listings.

8. You'll have fewer expiring listings. When you effectively service your listings, you will get maximum results in minimum time. Your properties will sell sooner and you will reduce the chances that the listing will expire.

9. You'll earn more referrals. Your satisfied sellers will become important centers of influence, which will help to build up your own lucrative business. People like to recommend those who have helped them.

10. In the end, you will enjoy a profitable real estate career. With more listings sold, you'll be free to move on, to devote more time to procuring more listings, which in turn will generate more sales and will ultimately make more money for you.

TECHNIQUES YOU CAN USE TO GAIN THESE BENEFITS

How to obtain correct and complete information

One common pitfall you'll want to avoid is accepting, as correct, information passed on to you by a seller or from a previous Multiple Listing brochure. If you do, some detrimental problems could develop. To avoid this, a good rule to follow is to carefully verify all data involved. This includes mortgage information, legal description, lot size, zoning, square footage of improvements, schools, ownership, and taxes. In addition, it is important to be specific and accurate in itemizing what is and what is not included with the property. If these appear correctly on the listing agreement, the brochure, and the purchase and sale contract, you'll prevent problems from arising due to omissions or errors.

You can get appropriate and reliable information regarding the property only from official sources, such as the deed, title policy, mortgage, public records, lending institutions, tax assessor's office, and school board.

Verifying mortgage information

It is vitally important for the buyer, the seller, and you to know if any of the following apply to the existing mortgage:

- Assumption special clauses—Prepayment penalties.
  - —Right to change the interest rate.
  - —Right to approve buyer.
  - —Any other special clauses or conditions.
- Variations on amounts of monthly payments.

A word of caution: Some sales have run into serious trouble because the seller and/or the lister said, "The mortgage is assumable," whereby both the agent and the selling agent *assumed* that it meant the original rate of interest, without any prepayment penalties, or without the mortgagee having the right to approve the buyer. Of course, this was often not the case. For the past few years, such special clauses have been appearing in mortgages. Mortgages are changing all the time. They affect assumption, method of payments, and number of years. Therefore, you'll be safe instead of sorry if you investigate the mortgage immediately following the signing of the listing agreement. A form letter you can use to request mortgage information is on page 116.

Checking legal description

If there is any discrepancy in the legal description or the lot size, complications and delays may arise. It pays to obtain correct information from an official source, such as a plat map, and then to check carefully for typographical errors wherever this information appears.

Procuring the latest tax information

Because taxes change from one year to another, you'll play it safe when you request the taxes on the property from the tax assessor's office and then designate the taxes as of the date on which you received the information.

Receiving information over the telephone

Whenever you receive any information on the telephone, it is most advisable to ask for the name and position of the person to whom you are speaking. Keep a record of it in your file, together with the date and the specific information you received. It is also a good policy, when getting mortgage information or specific details concerning the closing, to confirm all points in writing.

Before leaving this phase of servicing the listing, I'd like to tell you about a particular listing I acquired. The house had been listed for $133,000. The listing expired. When I checked the information on the brochure the seller handed me, I discovered that there were five errors. The taxes were $1000 more, monthly payments were $51.00 more, mortgage balance was $700.00 less, 4-ton central air and heat had been omitted, and the name of the owner was incorrect. (The deed of the property was actually recorded in the name of the seller's attorney as Trustee for the seller and his wife.)

Errors such as these will be detected and corrected when you carefully verify the facts on each of your listings.

Request for Mortgage Information*

(It is very important to use this form so that all information is accurate. Send to existing mortgagees.)

Date _____

Gentlemen:

We have just been designated as Agent to sell the following house: (Complete this section and mail to mortgagee.)

Address: _____

Legal: _____

Owner: _____

Mortgage co.: _____

Address _____

Mortgage loan no.: _____

May I please have the following information:

Present mortgage balance _____

Interest rate _____ %

Term of mortgage _____

Name of insurance agent: _____

Is there a prepayment penalty? _____

           ☐ Yes   ☐ with qualifying

Can this mortgage be assumed? ____ ☐ No   ☐ without qualifying

Is there an acceleration clause? _____

Monthly payment _____

Is there an escrow account? _____ If so, any shortage? _____

Where is the abstract stored? _____

Partial _____ Complete _____

The property is being placed on the market for sale.

Cordially,

_____ , Associate
(Name of real estate firm)

I hereby authorize the release of the above information.

_____
Seller

_____

*Reprinted from the *Associates Handbook,* with the permission of the Associates Committee of the Miami Board of Realtors.

Listing what is included and what is excluded

Misunderstandings and disputes frequently develop over such items as chandeliers, air-conditioning units, appliances, book-cases, or wall brackets. You'll avoid these problems if, on the listing agreement, you carefully itemize all of the items which the seller agrees will stay and the items which will not stay with the property; identify these items with brand names and serial numbers, if possible; and include this information on both the brochure and the contract for sale and purchase.

The difference between a smooth sale and one with problems is usually in direct proportion to how complete and accurate the information is that you present regarding your listing.

A mortgage broker told me that one of the most common complaints comes from buyers who discover after moving in that such items as refrigerators, washers, or dryers were not the ones they saw when they viewed the house. The seller had substituted an inferior appliance. The buyer blames everyone, but most of all he blames the real estate agent who sold him the house. The broker commented that if real estate salespeople would only identify the appliances, this would not happen.

Advertising media

There are two major methods readily available for you to use to attract prospects for your listings. One is a Multiple Listing Service, for which you prepare a brochure aimed at exciting other agents, so that they too will be eager to show and sell your listing. The other method, of course, is advertising in magazines and newspapers, directing your copy toward making the phone ring with inquiries. People call because the house you described sounds like what they are looking for.

The next step, after you have assembled information that is as complete and accurate as possible, is to present these facts briefly and in a most appealing manner. While you are preparing the write-up for Multiple Listing, you should also write two or three power-pulling ads. You're bound to get the best results then, while the details are fresh in your mind and you're still enthusiastic about your newest listing.

Merchandising creatively

We all know that it takes time to write clever, catchy, effective real estate ads. But what many real estate salespeople do not know is that being creative does not necessarily mean being original. I have learned to borrow other people's ideas, and to adapt catchy headings and picturesque words to my own ads. The object, of course, is to make the advertising dollars invested and the time spent work to move the property fast. So I found that it does pay to paraphrase cleverly. I'm sure that you will too.

Moreover, if you treat each listing as if it is the only one you will ever get, then you will surely be diligent in devoting whatever time is necessary to think of clever ways to let everyone know about your listing. With that attitude, you'll be determined to get it sold quickly, and chances are you will.

Key rules for writing power-pulling ads

To help you in writing effective ads, here are some important rules:

> *Promise.* In the heading, offer a buyer's benefit, one which attracts attention and arouses curiosity to read on.

- Example: "More for Your Money"

> *Prove It.* Follow the idea through, using picture words. *Briefly* describe benefits and features to satisfy the desires and needs of the people who will live there.

- Example: "Rambling rustic 3 bedroom 2 bath Rancher nestled among estates of over $100,000, beamed living room with wood-burning fireplace, charming kitchen and breakfast area, central air and heat."

> *Push.* End with a strong closer, one that impels the reader to take action now, to want to see and buy at once.

- Example: "Location right, price more so! Only $72,500."

A few helpful hints

- *Include price.* Research proves that ads are more effective when the price is mentioned.
- *Be honest.* Avoid exaggerating—it removes doubt and suspicion.
- *Finally...* write as though you were talking to someone who is looking for a home, enumerating all outstanding benefits and appealing features. Then cut, condense, sift out, and select the "hot buttons," those items that will turn on buyers for that particular house.

What response are you getting from your ads?

When you check the records of the results of your ads, you may be either surprised or disappointed. Sometimes, what you considered to be a dynamic ad might pull, while at other times, it might not work at all. Results may vary on different days, at different times of the year, for different types of houses, and in different areas. Nevertheless, from the records you keep, you will probably be able to reach some conclusions that will guide you accordingly.

Whatever the results are, your seller will be pleased that you are keeping him informed of what is transpiring. In fact, he may even surprise you and contribute some new ideas that could be the "clinchers" you need.

One further suggestion: Whenever you come across particularly effective words or phrases, keep them in a file for constant reference. Sometimes a salesperson uses an idea that pulls, then gets busy, goes on to other things, and completely forgets to use this super idea again.

How to explain marketing procedures to the seller

After the property is listed, action begins when you inform your seller about marketing procedures. In order to make sure that you cover the main points, it is helpful to have on hand two checklists: one to explain what you will be taking care of, and the other noting what will be expected of the owner.

Whatever you plan to do, let the seller know. For instance, tell him that you will:

- Have a "For Sale" sign put on the property.
- Obtain extra keys; one for yourself, one for the office.
- Notify your office staff of the listing and arrange an office caravan on a date suitable to the seller. (It's advisable to explain the details of a caravan—the purpose and how your office does it.)
- Prepare all information immediately for the Multiple Listing Service.
- Notify the Multiple Listing Service of the date and time, convenient to the seller, for holding the house open for inspection by other brokers.
- Arrange with the owner and notify the newspaper of dates for holding the house open to the public.

- Deliver a copy of the Multiple Listing brochure as soon as it appears.
- Prepare three ads while preparing the brochure.
- Send to the mortgage company an estoppel letter, a payoff statement for the existing mortgage.
- Collect the cards of cooperating salespeople who show the house and check with them for comments.
- Report regularly to the owner. Share with him the activity as well as any lack of activity.

The seller's role

As his concerned listing agent, you should explain to the seller that it takes teamwork to get the property sold. Make him aware of his role—what you expect him to do and why:

- *Have the house ready for showing.* Explain that the house can have a lived-in look, yet should be neat and tidy so that it will be appealing to those who view it.
- *Free the house of unpleasant odors.* Many buyers are turned off by the smell of animals or tobacco.
- *Arrange for pets to be confined or removed to a place where they will not interfere with the showing.*
- *Remove or substitute such items as chandeliers or other fixtures that the seller does not intend to remain with the house.* Explain that this will avoid serious problems that might otherwise come up later on, because buyers usually want and insist on having those fixtures that they see in the house.
- *Spruce up the exterior to give a good first impression.* Neatly trim lawns, shrubs, and trees. In the winter, clear the walks of ice and snow.
- *Make any recommended repairs.* These are generally minor. Explain that little things often make a big difference in getting a better price or a quicker sale. These things might include replacing high-wattage bulbs in fixtures to brighten up dark areas, repairing holes in screens, fixing dripping faucets, replacing cracked windows, painting water-marked ceilings, or washing off spots on walls and woodwork.
- *Prior to the showing,* turn on the lights, open the drapes and curtains to give the rooms a bright look, turn off the TV but turn on soft, stereo music for background as is done in model houses and condominiums.

- *Finally, whenever the house is being shown, the family should be absent or inconspicuous.* Explain that buyers talk more freely when they may not be overheard. Some sellers think that they should be on hand to answer questions that may arise. Warn the seller about the perils of doing so. Tell him that, from experience, you know that the seller's presence hinders rather than helps any sale. In their anxiety to help, the sellers invariably talk too much or introduce information that becomes objections and, in the end, kills the sale. This is a good point at which to relate a specific incident which will emphasize this point. Explain to the seller that, as his agent, it is your job to sell the house. That is what you are trained to do and what he hired you to do.

How the seller's interference triggered a buyer's resistance

Here is a classic example of what can happen when a seller voluntarily visits with a prospect who is seriously considering buying his home. It happened one Sunday when the sellers returned home 15 minutes before the closing time of their "open house."

An Army sergeant and his wife had completed a tour of the house and were very favorably impressed. We were making final arrangements to draw up a contract. In walked the owners, Mr. and Mrs. R. They were introduced and lingered on. Sgt. G., mostly out of politeness, asked some simple questions about how the filter system in the pool worked. Mr. R. seized the opportunity to answer. Excitedly, he went on and on in great detail, continuing to ramble for about 10 or 15 minutes. As soon as he could get a word in edgewise, Sgt. G. thanked him. He and Mrs. G. left immediately.

Outside, Sgt. G. told me, "We were all set to go ahead, but now I don't know. I'm suspicious that Mr. R. tried too hard to convince us that the pool and the filtering system were fine. Now I have my doubts. I really think something must be wrong. We'd like to look at some other houses."

The magic moment seemed lost. It took a lot of talking on my part to get the G.'s to reconsider. Finally, I assured them that they could be certain that the pool and filtering system would be in working order because they themselves could choose the licensed companies to do the inspections, all of which would be included in their contract to protect them. Although this seemed to satisfy them, they still remained suspicious about every detail throughout the sale. Those few moments, in which Mr. R. volunteered a lengthy answer to a simple question, were enough to almost kill the sale.

You may have had similar experiences with sellers who either did not understand or did not play their role as the silent selling partner. When you narrate stories such as this to a seller who has just listed his house, it should make enough of an impression so that he'll remember not to interfere and will willingly leave the selling to you and the other cooperating salespeople.

Fulfilling your promise to report regularly

At the listing interview, you promised your seller that you would not be like some of the other agents who disappear after the listing agreement is signed. Later, when you explained the procedures of processing the listing, you told him again that you would report regularly and keep him informed of what was or was not happening. He expects you to back up these promises with deeds. You will want to keep records and let him know the results of the ads, open houses, and showings. These reports can be brief summaries, but should conclude with a positive remark. For instance, you could say, "Only three people showed up today for the open house, but as you know, it isn't the number that counts. All we need is one as long as it is the right one." Or, "We had plenty of response to the ad, but most of the callers are just lookers, rather than serious buyers. I know you wouldn't want me to bring anyone to look at your house who did not seem to be a serious prospect, would you?" By accenting the positive and minimizing the negative in this fashion, you will help pave the way toward getting an extension on the listing if that is necessary.

Extending the listing before it expires

You have worked hard, spent some money, and invested a great deal of time in this listing. Even though you have been conscientious in servicing it, besides having good rapport with the seller, it would be a mistake to take it for granted that he will automatically extend the listing agreement. To ensure getting an extension, you should visit with the seller a few weeks before the listing is due to expire and ask him to sign the necessary forms. Explain to him that it takes time to process the paper work.

There should be no problem and you'll be safe. The papers will be processed on time and you will avoid any complications. However, you should be prepared just in case the seller surprises you and is hesitant or reluctant to extend the listing. If this should occur, try asking some questions about whether there is anything you or your company are doing that he is unhappy with, whether you are doing all of the things you promised you would do, and if there is anything he would like you to do differently. If there don't seem to be any complaints, review from the file what has transpired so far. Tell him that you also have an investment of time and money in the listing, and that you would like to protect that investment. Then, enthusiastically present one or two new ideas to further promote the sale. These might include some new ads, or your plan to write up a new brochure. Let him know that, from experience, you have found that a new brochure is treated like a brand new listing and usually generates more activity. Tell him that it does take time to prepare and process a brochure, and that is why you need the go-ahead now.

That extra bit of service

Whenever an associate contacts you about showing one of your listings, it is wise to present the details in an exciting and interesting fashion. In addition, ask him to please let you know the reaction of his customer, as well as his own. If he doesn't call you with his response, you should call him. This can prove vital to a sale. Not only will you learn of any objections, but you may find out that the customer showed some interest, in which case you can clarify some of the information, or call the agent's attention to some important features he overlooked, or perhaps suggest terms that might be appropriate. It also makes good sense at this time to feed the other agent information on some of your other listings. These listings might be just what this associate needs for some of his other prospects.

Keeping in touch after the sale

Even though his seller may appear to be happy and relieved when he has accepted an offer to purchase, the smart salesperson continues to serve. Regardless of how competently you are handling the closing process, you will keep your seller apprised of what is transpiring and of who is doing what. When you do this, it will help to maintain the good relationship you worked so hard to establish. And, to show his appreciation, your seller will be happy to comply with your request for a testimonial letter verifying his satisfaction with the excellent service you rendered.

In a nutshell

As Lord Chesterfield so wisely commented, "Whatever is worth doing at all, is worth doing well." This is very true of listing property. If you secure a saleable listing, it is worth pursuing and properly servicing. You owe it to your seller, to your profession, and to yourself to fulfill your obligation to promote and service each and every listing to the best of your ability.

Checklist for Effectively Servicing the Listing

Do you take some positive steps when you start servicing the listing?

Procure and verify the facts and figures pertaining to the property, including legal description, present taxes, existing mortgages, lot size, zoning, square footage, improvements, schools, ownership?

Do you send a mortgage loan letter to verify important information such as:

Assumption special clauses (prepayment penalties, right to change interest rate, right to approve buyer, other conditions)?

Variations on amounts of monthly payments?

Do you keep records of all information received by phone and confirm it in writing, including the date and the name of the person giving the information?

Do you devote a certain amount of time to presenting the property in the most accurate and appealing manner?

Immediately write two or three power-pulling ads?

Use a promise in the heading?

Back it up in the ad?

Include the price?

Condense?

Keep a file of the best-selling words?

Check to see if the ad made the phone ring?

Inform the seller of the results?

Avoid misunderstandings by noting on the brochure all items included and excluded?

Do you strive to establish a satisfactory partner relationship with your seller?

Use a checklist to explain your responsibility?

Use a checklist to explain the seller's role?

Report regularly to the seller regarding activity and lack of activity, all the while accentuating the positive? Continue reporting after the sale until the sale is finalized?

Do you work closely with other agents when they inquire about your listing?

Do you request and get an extension before the listing expires?

Follow up on buyer hesitancy?

Review activities?

Present one or two new ideas?

Do you feel that you service every listing you are responsible for to the best of your ability?

10

The Serious Mistake of

Overpricing

the Property

When an overpriced listing appears on the market, everyone involved is adversely affected, including the Realtor, the listing agent, and the seller himself. Judging from the great number of expired listings and the number of listings that remain on the market for a long period of time, it is evident that many salespeople are accepting listings that are far in excess of their competitive market value. Why does an agent do this? Generally, it is because he's hungry for listings or because he is not fully aware of the dangers involved.

"The secret," says Realtor Len O. Holloway, "is to place yourself in enough listing situations so that you aren't desperate for it at any price. A *sold* listing is your best advertisement. An *expired* is your worst and may tarnish your reputation."

At times, you may find yourself influenced by a zealous seller. The following situation illustrates what can happen when a seller insists on getting an unrealistic price on his home, and an agent succumbs.

How a high price was paid for an overpriced listing

This seller was a typical greedy homeowner. He insisted on an asking price of $135,000, completely ignoring the comparative market analysis, which indicated $120,000 as absolutely the top price. As luck would have it, an offer of $120,000 actually did come in within the first three weeks of the listing period, but the seller promptly turned it down. He flatly refused to make a counteroffer. After that, the house just sat and sat without another offer. At the end of six months, the listing expired. It was listed again with another broker, still at $135,000. Meanwhile, the seller moved out of town. For another five months, mortgage payments continued along with other expenses, including taxes, insurance, and gardeners. Finally, because of these mounting expenses and fear of vandalism, the seller became desperate and felt forced to accept the low sum of $99,500.

This was a tremendous loss all around. The first listing agent received no compensation at all for his six months of work or the expenses he incurred for advertising. And the unfortunate seller lost $20,500 plus eleven months of expenses for upkeep. Costly mistakes like this can be avoided if the property is priced reasonably.

THE BENEFITS YOU'LL GAIN

1. You'll develop mutual trust and confidence between yourself and your seller. When you show him that you are genuinely sincere in attempting to get the best price for him, he'll realize that you aim to help him, not harm him.

2. You'll earn the seller's respect and admiration. When you speak out frankly and honestly, the seller becomes aware that you are giving him the facts and not just painting rosy pictures simply to get the listing.

3. The seller will know that you are not just anxious to have the listing. He'll understand that you're not taking what might seem to him to be the easy way out, but instead that you are primarily interested in getting his house sold.

4. The seller will believe you. Statistics about current market conditions and prices that you present convince him of the advisability of listing his home at the realistic price you recommend.

5. You'll earn the reputation of being a good lister. It won't take long before word gets around in the marketplace that you have an inventory of well-priced listings.

6. You'll enjoy the cooperation of other associates. They'll help sell your listings. Smart salespeople prefer to work with "the cream of the crop." They'll pick your realistically priced listing to show their customers.

7. You'll rid yourself of unnecessary frustrations. Knowing that you have properly priced the listing, you'll be mentally free to concentrate on moving it fast. You'll avoid concern about mounting expenses and wasting valuable time, or worrying about how to get a sizeable price reduction in a desperate effort to salvage the listing.

8. You'll greatly increase your listing power. People love to deal with and recommend successful people. Your "Sold" signs serve as a magnet to attract others who might be thinking of selling their homes. They'll feel that they, too, can rely on you to move their properties for them.

9. Your listings will sell, not expire. As Realtors always say, "A listing properly priced is half sold."

10. Consequently, you'll earn much more money. You'll also earn it in less time. This is the natural course of events when you list and sell more properties, sell them sooner, and have fewer of them expire. You're bound to be a winner!

TECHNIQUES YOU CAN USE TO GAIN THESE BENEFITS

Convincing the seller through comparables

For most homeowners, pricing a home is a dilemma. A seller may make inquiries about some of the houses in his neighborhood that have sold recently or are presently up for sale. He may not always get correct answers. Then he may talk to various real estate salespeople who offer different opinions and confuse him further. Of course, the seller is anxious to aim for the absolute top dollar. But it is the unprofessional real estate agent who will take unfair advantage of him by deliberately recommending a greatly inflated price and assuring the seller that he can actually get that price for him. He may even go one step further and say that he already has a buyer for that particular house. It is a great injustice to mislead a seller in this way just to get the listing. The true professional behaves differently. He is honest and he does not suggest an inflated price, nor does he volunteer a price off the top of his head. Instead, he shows the owner, by means of comparables, what the property should bring, and convinces him that it is the best possible figure at that time and that it is realistic.

When discussing the price, it is best to first agree with the seller and then proceed: "Mr. Homeowner, I understand how you feel. I can appreciate that you want to get as much as you can for the sale of your home, and you should. That's exactly what I would like to do for you. It is for that reason that I'd like to explain why it is important for you to review a comparative market analysis before you arrive at a price. This analysis does take time to prepare, but it is the only fair way for you to compare properties."

You can then continue: "There's still another matter I'd like to call to your attention. And that is, who actually sets the price? Although we know that appraisers are trained to determine the *value* of property, they do not determine the *price*. Regardless of the value, it is the *buyer* who ultimately sets the price. It isn't what you or I *think* your house is worth that counts, it is what some buyer out there is willing to pay for your home at this time. It is simply a matter of supply and demand.

"It's very much like buying stock. Do you own any stocks, Mr. Homeowner, or are you familiar with them? Let's take, for example, AT&T. Do you agree that this is a good, sound company? Is there any doubt at all about the enormous volume of business they are doing and will continue to do in the future? (Everyone readily agrees that it's one of the largest and soundest corporations in America.) Are you aware that in the mid-60s you could have bought shares of AT&T for as much as $75.00 per share, and that if you decided to sell your shares in 1977, the best price you could receive would have been $65.00? The reason for this is that, although AT&T is a top quality stock and the company is one of the corporate giants, the stock is like all stocks—the price is set by supply and demand at the time of the sale. It is the same in selling real estate—supply and demand are the determining factors in setting price.

"That is why, Mr. Homeowner, to guide yourself in making your decision, it is important to look at today's market, at what people are paying now for homes similar to yours. This will give you an idea of what you can expect."

Property properly priced is half sold

You have shown the seller the facts and figures revealing the activity of sales in his neighborhood. This includes dates and prices of recently sold properties and properties still available for sale. To be more specific and graphic, you can show a few examples—write-ups or brochures—of properties that you or your office have sold quickly because the price was right. Then, for contrast, you can show some other listings that have expired or have been on the market for a long time mainly because they were overpriced. Of course, when you pick houses that are similar to the seller's it will be much more effective. It becomes evident to the seller that what you are saying does occur. He can identify with the situation. You might add that he can probably appreciate what Realtors already know—that buyers won't buy greatly overpriced homes, sellers can't sell them, and smart salespeople avoid them like the plague.

It is well to remind the seller that the greatest activity on any listing occurs when it first appears on the market. If he capitalizes on this, and if his house is priced right, it's already half sold when the listing hits the market. Persuade him to take advantage of getting off to a great start.

Giving honest projections of possible pitfalls

The following is a list of some truisms. It includes pitfalls that your seller should be cognizant of and should want to avoid. For convenience, you might want to have such a list in front of you to check the items off with your seller, or you might even leave it with him as a reminder.

THE PERILS OF OVERPRICING*

1. The best time to sell for the highest price is when the house is *new* on the market. *Overpricing* causes you to lose this valuable period. You cannot recapture later—your house is only new once on the market.

2. The *wrong* people look at the house, if any at all. People not only *often buy* in price ranges, they *look* in price ranges also. Chances

---

*Used by permission of Len O. Holloway, Realtor, Coral Gables, Florida.

are the right buyer will never see it. $50,000 buyers won't look at $70,000 homes.

3. Other *cooperating salesmen* don't want to lose credibility with their buyers by showing them *overpriced* listings.

4. Other Realtors know from experience that *fair* offers are *usually* rejected on overpriced houses.

5. Some buyers are often embarrassed or reluctant to make offers considerably below the *overpriced* listing.

6. The house may become *shopworn*. Others begin to assume there is something *wrong* with the house.

7. Only *lowball* offers are likely to come in. When people see that the house has been on the market for a long period, they think they can get a *bargain*.

8. The end result is that the sellers may end up with far *less* after a frustrating period than if they had priced the house at *fair market value* in the first place.

Discussing terms

While you are discussing price, it is also a good time to make the seller aware that price is not the only thing that makes a sale. Most people do not realize that terms can be equally as important and sometimes even more so in completing the sale.

Explain to the seller that the various kinds of financing he will consider can make a difference. For instance, he may not know that FHA or VA financing are great ways to attract some buyers and can make the house more saleable. Another alternative might be for the seller to finance the house himself by taking back the full mortgage or taking back a second mortgage where there is an attractive, assumable, existing first mortgage. The buyer likes this opportunity to save closing costs. If a buyer should offer all cash, then the seller might be receptive to accepting a lesser price because he would be assured of a quick, easy sale, with no delays and no qualifying. He might find this attractive and worthwhile for him to consider.

Let the seller know that price is not the only item that may require negotiating. There are other important matters such as occupancy, items of personal property, or special conditions. Once a seller realizes that the main consideration in consummating a sale is not necessarily price alone, but often terms or the combination of price and terms, then he'll probably be more flexible about the price.

When to get a price reduction

Before talking about price reduction, I'd like to say that if the seller is strongly motivated and you know that he must sell, there's really little risk in taking the listing, even if it is overpriced. The seller's circumstances will dictate his actions. Hence, he'll most likely be amenable to an early price adjustment. And, when it comes time to negotiate, he'll be forced to accept a reasonable offer. In his position he simply can't afford to do otherwise.

The best time to get a price adjustment is within the first month. If you wait until the listing is about to expire, it will be too late. The house will already be shopworn.

Actually, you should begin asking for a price adjustment at the listing interview when price is discussed. At that time, if the seller insists on a price that you feel is too high, explain that you are willing to go along with his request in order to test the market. However, let him know that you'll do so on the condition that if you do set the price he is suggesting, and if you do all of the things you said you would (such as putting the house on Multiple Listing, giving it complete exposure, holding it open, and advertising), and if not a single offer comes in within the first three weeks, he'll be willing to adjust the price accordingly. Make sure that he agrees.

How to get a price adjustment

Since you previously planted the seeds for getting the necessary price adjustment, it is usually just a routine matter to go back three or four weeks later and get it. To remind the seller, you might say, "Mr. Homeowner, you do recall, don't you, that when we originally discussed the price you said you wanted to test the market, and you agreed that if I did all the things I said I would (enumerate again), and if no offers came through during the first three or four weeks, you would agree to make the necessary price adjustment to get your house sold?"

Then continue: "Mr. Homeowner, we know that your home is in good condition, that it has been widely exposed, and that it has been shown frequently. Yet, we have not received one offer. This can only mean one thing: the price is too high. I'm sure you'll agree that it's time to adjust the price. This is what we need to do now in order to get your house sold."

The seller usually understands and readily consents. If he does not, it may require more effort on your part. People don't always remember, so you may have to review the updated comparables with him, as well as the important points you covered a few weeks earlier during the original listing interview. It may even take some additional visits and polite persistence on your part to make the seller realize the serious hazards of continuing to keep his house listed at a price well above that which the current market indicates is reasonable.

A motivated seller will generally comply with your request. However, if the seller is not sufficiently motivated and continues to be stubborn, you should recognize that you are working for a poor employer. You'll be better off if you chalk it off as a learning experience and move on to more cooperative employers.

Why not start off with a higher price and come down later?

Most sellers have a difficult time understanding why you aren't at least willing to start off with a higher price to give it a try. You can always come down later. Tell such a seller that you know how he feels, but it just doesn't work that way. You know from experience that most of the activity takes place within the first few weeks of the listing. Once this opportunity is lost, you cannot recapture it. You might add: "Mr. Homeowner, you may not realize it, but if you overprice your home, you're not really putting it on the market, you're taking it off."

To a seller who wants to start out in the beginning with a high price, or to the seller who thinks he's not in a rush, you might relate a story like the one at the beginning of this chapter—a story about a seller who paid a large penalty for overpricing his property. You might choose to tell him a story about a seller in his neighborhood, or about another house in the same price range and category, that ran into serious problems because of overpricing. The seller will identify with the situation you relate.

In the end, you'll win

If you follow the guidelines offered here and use the techniques suggested, you won't be cluttering up your inventory with unsaleable properties. Instead, you will devote your time and effort exclusively to listings that are promising and productive. You'll discover that everyone will benefit—the Realtor, the buyer, the seller, and especially you, the listing agent. You'll end up with much more money in your pocket.

Checklist for Preventing the Overpricing of the Property

Do you use fair and appropriate comparables with the seller to set a realistic price?

Persuade the seller of their value?

Explain to the seller who actually sets the price in a way he understands?

Reinforce your price recommendation and satisfy the seller with visual proof of quick sales and troubled sales in similar situations?

Discuss the importance of also considering terms that can produce sales?

At the time of listing, do you have the owner agree to an early price adjustment if necessary?

Follow through and easily obtain an early price adjustment?

Do you mistakenly succumb to the seller's suggestion to start off with a much higher price and come down later?

11

Losing

Control of the Selling Process

The meeting was set for 8:30 a.m., at my seller's new palatial estate. Andy, a salesman from another office, was to present an offer of over $100,000 on the seller's former home. Because Andy was newly licensed and timid, he asked me to please do him the favor of presenting his offer for him.

Mrs. Z. led us into an enormously impressive study, and then requested a copy of the contract, saying that her husband would look it over while he ate his breakfast.

Andy was ready to hand it over. But I was not about to lose control. In a polite, but firm tone, I responded, "Oh, no. We don't mind. We'll be glad to wait until Mr. Z. has finished his breakfast and then we can all go over it together."

It worked like a charm. A few minutes later, Mr. Z. joined us with a respectful, cooperative, almost docile attitude. Continuing to maintain control, I directed the seating arrangement at the table and proceeded with the presentation in a planned order, without any interruptions.

By setting the tone, I made negotiating easier for all of us. As a result, we were able to arrive at a reasonable counteroffer that was also acceptable to the buyer.

THE BENEFITS YOU'LL GAIN

1. You'll be the one who determines when, how, and what to do. You'll be in charge.
2. You'll be able to stick to the essentials and avoid drifting off in discussions of irrelevant matters.
3. You'll guide the conversation in a productive direction. You'll have the advantage.
4. Buyers, sellers, fellow associates, attorneys, and others will respect your actions. They'll respond favorably.
5. The parties concerned will follow your instructions.
6. You'll gain your clients' support and cooperation.
7. You'll control the properties when you work exclusively on "exclusives." You'll decide how to merchandise them effectively and you'll be both protected and paid when they're sold.
8. All of this means that you'll be selling on purpose, not by accident.
9. From contract to closing, you'll win through control, not by intimidation.

TECHNIQUES YOU CAN USE TO GAIN THESE BENEFITS

The key to control—planning ahead

Because real estate selling is made up of a series of little sales which eventually lead up to the final sale, it is important to control each individual step. These steps are the eight selling situations discussed in Chapter 1: 1) making appointments, 2) listing interviews, 3) writing ads and brochures, 4) answering incoming calls, 5) showing properties, 6) presenting offers and counteroffers, 7) closing sales, and 8) processing sold properties.

The best strategy for controlling each of these situations, and one that will help you to feel secure and confident, is to arm yourself with the necessary ammunition. That consists of preparing the appropriate information, facts, forms, checklists, and supplies. Being prepared will permit you to be the leader. You will be ready to cover whatever contingencies may arise. You're not likely to fumble or lose control, because you will have the information on hand. When you are dealing from strength of authority and knowledge, it's easy to lead the other person in every selling situation.

How to set the stage

When you consider that each selling situation constitutes a performance in itself, it is easy to understand why you need to set the stage in each and every step, thus ensuring a top performance. To do this, arrange the seating where it is best for you, where you can watch the reactions of the other parties, and where it is comfortable and convenient for you to handle your papers. In a home, suggest sitting at a table. On a listing interview, you might say, "May we please sit at a table where it will be convenient to write down the details about your home?" When presenting an offer, you might ask, "May we sit at a table where it will be convenient to show you the information I have?"

After you arrange the seating so that you are facing your prospects, you can watch their facial expressions without moving your head back and forth like a Ping-Pong spectator.

When you take charge and direct the seating in this professional manner, you will not only put yourself in the most advantageous position, but you will also gain the attention and respect of your clients. Your buyers or sellers will then be in a responsive mood, ready to listen to whatever you have to present.

Tested tips for controlling real estate selling situations

Concentrate on pertinent information. When a buyer or seller asks a simple question for information, you will frequently find yourself getting carried away with long, detailed answers. This is a common mistake real estate salespeople make. For instance, a prospect asks the price, and a salesman responds by describing the neighborhood, the schools, and the whole house. Or a homeowner asks what commission the company charges, and the agent delivers a long dissertation on the service he offers, the merits of his firm, performance records, and the advertising policy. You should always refrain from adding any information that is not relevant to the question. In other words, answer as briefly as possible, stick to the point, and get right back to the business at hand. When you do this, you will not only maintain control of the situation, but you won't run the risk of losing your customer either.

Avoid being sidetracked. Whatever the selling situation, it is easy to go off in other directions, discussing interesting but irrelevant topics. Some prospects either intentionally or accidentally wander away from the subject at hand, leading you off-course. As a result, various things can happen to slow down the progress of the selling process, or even kill the sale, such as a) your prospect's mind is diverted by bits of information you have given him, b) you antagonize him because of a difference of opinion, c) obstacles arise from discussing extraneous subjects, or d) you run out of time before you have completed the task of getting the listing or selling the house.

By keeping your prospect on a planned course, you'll take him on a direct route to the desired destination—a sale or a listing.

Handle interruptions. You may be making good progress with your prospects, and they may be agreeing with you that this is the house for them. Then you say, "Let's put the details down on paper," and just as you're about to start writing, the phone rings. You take the call. Meanwhile, your buyers look at each other and whisper. When you're through with the call, they thank you, but say that they have to leave, that they have changed their minds, or that they want to look at some more houses before making a final decision. The spell is broken. That magic moment might also be lost when an associate interrupts to ask you a question. Any interruption slows down the selling process and is often fatal to the sale.

To prevent such interruptions, you can make the following announcement: "Please hold all of my calls. I do not wish to be disturbed while Mr. and Mrs. Prospect are here." This flatters Mr. and Mrs. Prospect, and puts them in a receptive mood. Most importantly, you have made certain that you can conduct your interview without any interruptions that could adversely affect your presentation.

This action takes care of controlling the situation in the office. However, when you're in a home, the usual distraction is the TV or radio. An easy way to take charge and prevent this is by merely requesting, "May we please turn off the TV?" The homeowner will do as you ask. He accepts the fact that you are there on serious business, and he will respectfully listen to what you have come to tell him.

Another kind of interruption that might disrupt your presentation occurs when your buyer or seller injects a question. If you ignore the question, he may be annoyed and will probably lose interest in what you are saying because he'll still be thinking about his unanswered question. On the other hand, if you get involved with the complete answer, you might drift away from the subject you are covering, or you might give information that it would be more advantageous to withhold until later. Therefore, to acknowledge the question and yet not lose the train of thought that you are pursuing, you can do the following:

- Answer politely with a "yes" or a "no": "Yes, Mr. Prospect, that is the way it works."

- Answer the question with a question, as discussed in Chapter 3. After a very brief explanation, you might conclude with something like, "Did I make myself clear?" and then continue with the presentation.

- Simply say, "That's a good question, Mr. Prospect," or, "I'm glad you asked that, Mr. Prospect. I do plan to cover that later on. To make sure I don't forget, I'll make a note of it right now." Write it down and proceed with your presentation. Before concluding the presentation, you might ask, "Did I answer all of your questions? Do you have any additional questions now?"

As you can see, when you handle interruptions correctly you minimize their disrupting effects and you still maintain control of the situation.

The magic power of the "change-the-subject" technique. The conversation starts to drift, your prospect doesn't seem to be paying attention, and you sense that you're losing control. Or, perhaps you are meeting resistance and all seems lost. At such times you can effectively use the technique of changing the subject. You might begin with, "by the way," or, "I thought you'd like to know," or, "what do you think of," and follow with a subject that is not directly related to the point you are covering.

Another excellent way to use this technique is to suggest a break for coffee, lunch, dinner, or even cocktails. In Chapter 5, there was a good example of how well this idea worked, when I invited my prospect and his family to lunch. That break was just what was needed then—it worked wonders.

When you change the subject, the other person has a sense of relief. The atmosphere also seems to change and it's like letting in a breath of fresh air. When you do return to the original subject, you can generally revive the other person's interest and continue.

How to overcome the "we'll call you" syndrome

When they make subsequent appointments, many salespeople seem to lose control. They permit the other person to say,

"We'll let you know what we decide," or, "We'll call you to set up an appointment." The agent waits and waits, sometimes neglecting other important matters. This is an unsatisfactory and frustrating arrangement. The other person is in control. When they say, "We'll call you," you can regain control by firmly taking charge and arranging then and there for another specific date and time. You can vary the wording, depending on the circumstances. You might say, "Since I am in and out of the office so much of the time, it's best to be certain and set up a convenient time right now for tomorrow or Wednesday," or, "It takes time, as you know, to line up properties, make the calls, arrange for picking up keys, and so on, so let's set up a definite time right now that we know will coincide with your schedule."

If, for some reason, a return phone call is necessary, merely ask, "What will be the best time to reach you, and where? Fine, then I'll call you tomorrow morning at your office before noon."

When you insist on a definite appointment or arrangement, *you* control the situation. Your prospect not only respects you, but he also recognizes that you are a professional and you take his business seriously.

Taking charge at listing interviews

With a planned presentation, you will be the one to control the interview. You arrange the seating, and decide what you want to discuss regarding your service and in what order you want to do it. As a result, the professional manner you display in conducting the interview makes a favorable impression on the sellers. You'll find them attentive and responsive.

Here is an example of the importance of being in command during the listing interview. This case involved the attorney for the sellers. I have found that some attorneys do try to intimidate real estate agents. However, you can apply this same principle in other selling situations.

How an attorney tried to take charge

A young couple at a listing interview said that selling their home was a new experience for them and that they would not sign the listing agreement until their attorney had looked it over.

I said, "Fine, let's get him on the phone."

I asked him if he was familiar with the Board of Realtors Multiple Listing agreement. He was, but he wanted me to insert a clause to the effect that we would advertise in the newspaper each week over a specified period.

Then, in a polite, cultured tone, I responded, "May I ask, sir, if there is anything legally incorrect about this agreement?"

"Oh, no. I was just offering some personal advice."

"Thank you very much, but Mr. and Mrs. Seller were primarily concerned about the legality of this agreement. That is what they wanted to know at this time."

That ended the discussion. Mr. and Mrs. Seller were satisfied. This was a simple case of winning through control, not by intimidation.

Maintaining control at the negotiating table

There is probably no time when you will find it more important to be prepared for contingencies that may arise than at the negotiating table. Although it may be difficult, maintaining control becomes a key factor in the outcome.

Selling agents frequently become intimidated by overprotective listers, interfering attorneys, greedy sellers, or thoughtless buyers. The following two cases are examples of ways to deal with overprotective listers.

How a selling agent refused to be intimidated and saved the sale

Karl, the lister, was an experienced manager of a large, popular real estate firm. He should have known better. The buyer, vice-president of a successful developing company of low-priced homes, was well-qualified to buy this $45,000 home. Before submitting his offer to purchase, he had previously contacted a well-known mortgage company with whom he had connections and had made arrangements for a four-week closing.

The first objection Karl raised was, "I know that 90 percent financing will be O.K., but I'm not sure about 95 percent." This did not concern the seller, Edward, who was also a builder of homes in the area.

The seller took a pen and was just about to sign the contract when Karl remarked, "Edward, I must remind you that your attorney said not to sign anything until he has looked it over."

At this point, I looked Edward straight in the eye and, in a slow, calm voice said, "Edward, this is a simple contract with no special terms. It is a regular Board of Realtors purchase and sale contract being used by over 2000 salespeople. Do you have any questions or doubts about the legality of this contract?"

Edward, with pen still in hand, retorted, "Oh, these attorneys have too much to say anyway," and he promptly signed the contract, much to Karl's disappointment.

I felt that I had won that sale through control. The following tale, however, is about a less fortunate selling agent who was intimidated by a listing agent and lost the sale.

How the selling agent lost control and lost a $90,000 sale

The house was new on the market. Martin, the selling agent, brought in an offer of $90,000, with a $4000 deposit. The balance was to be all cash at closing. The buyer, an airline pilot, was a person of substance.

There was no problem about price. But Nora, the lister, a domineering individual, insisted that the sellers should not accept anything less than a 10 percent deposit. This meant an additional $5000. Without any discussion, the sellers followed her instructions and countered accordingly.

The buyer became very annoyed and rejected the counteroffer, saying that it was a matter of principle. He flatly refused to add anything to his initial deposit and the sale fell through.

Let's analyze this example. What could Martin have done? He could have taken charge and, in a professional manner, reminded the sellers that his buyer was not only ready and willing, but also very able to buy. He could have assured the sellers that the buyer's intent was genuine and then asked the sellers what possible risk there could be. Would anyone want to deliberately forfeit as much as $4000? Had Martin made certain that the sellers agreed on each point as he went along, then chances are he would have convinced the sellers and they would have overlooked Nora's advice. They would probably have accepted the contract as submitted. By taking command, Martin would not have permitted Nora to intimidate him.

Although it would have been unlikely, let's assume that the sellers remained stubborn in demanding a full 10 percent deposit. Martin still had another opportunity to regain control and save the sale, this time by influencing his buyer. First, he could have agreed with the buyer that the sellers were being unreasonable. Then, he could have reviewed the buyer's situation in a positive vein, by reminding him that this home was exactly what he and his wife wanted, with a large, lovely pool and beautifully landscaped grounds, all in the neighborhood they preferred. He could have continued to remind the buyers that they had admitted that raising the $5000 was really no problem, and that since it was to be an early closing, the additional money would have to be paid soon anyway. In view of this, and to simplify matters, it would be practical to increase the deposit now instead of a few weeks later and be happy knowing that they'd have the home they really wanted. With such an approach, chances are the buyer would have conceded. Martin would have regained control and most likely would have made the sale.

Instead, Martin returned to his buyer feeling very upset and annoyed by Nora's actions. He accepted his buyer's point of view. He made no attempt to regain control, thereby losing out on his second opportunity.

Wrapping it up

When you control a situation, it does not mean that you dominate it. Being assertive is not synonymous with being aggressive. Assertiveness is acceptable behavior, whereas aggressiveness is offensive and obnoxious. In selling real estate, one associates the word *aggressive* with high pressure and this is certainly most undesirable.

When you use control in a professional manner, as discussed in this chapter, you will earn the respect and cooperation of others and you will become proficient in obtaining satisfactory results in each situation.

Follow the guidelines given here and you'll be the leader. You'll be the one to take charge and you won't be intimidated.

Checklist for Control of the Selling Process

Do you begin exercising control by having all of the facts, figures, forms, and tools ready to cover each selling situation?

Making the appointment?

Selling the seller at the listing interview?

> Writing ads and brochures?
> Answering incoming telephone calls?
> Showing the property?
> Negotiating with the buyer and the seller?
> Closing the sale?
> Processing the sold property?

Do you determine and direct the seating arrangement to suit your needs?

Do you use field tested methods to maintain control?

> Avoid long, detailed answers to questions?
> Stay with the subject at hand?
> Handle interruptions tactfully, yet firmly?
> Have your calls held?
> Request turning off TV or radio?

Do you have a plan ready to take care of disrupting questions?

> Answer politely with "yes" or "no"?
> Answer with a question?
> Acknowledge the question and when you'll answer it, or make note of it for later?

Do you change the subject when they seem to be losing interest?

> Suggest a break?

Do you have a good response to their suggesting, "I'll call you"?

Do you feel that you favorably impress the seller at the listing interview with your professionalism?

> At the negotiating table?

Do you find your "take-charge" attitude earns respect and instills confidence in both buyer and seller?

Do you win each time by controlling the selling situation, rather than losing by being intimidated by the other person?

12

Failing to
Show the Property Effectively

Sometime ago I heard an interesting story about a man who looked at a very expensive diamond, was considering buying it, but decided not to. On his way out, the jewelry store manager asked him to please return for a moment. The manager took the same diamond and held it up to the light, very slowly turning it, showing off the magnificent, multi-brilliant facets. The customer's eyes lit up in admiration. As the manager gently placed the diamond on the black velvet pad before them, the man exclaimed, "I'll take it!"

Before departing, the customer hesitated, turned to the manager, and said, "I'm curious. Tell me something. A few moments ago, I was prepared to walk out of here without purchasing this beautiful diamond. Yet, it seemed so easy to buy it from you. How come?"

The manager replied, "The salesman who first showed you the diamond happens to *know* more about diamonds than probably anyone else in the world. But I *love* them."

The same is true of showing houses. It isn't enough just to know the details of each home you present. What you need is that added essential ingredient—showmanship. Just as the jeweler dramatized the beauty of the diamond, you can dramatize the features and benefits of a house in order to excite and emotionally involve your buyers.

THE BENEFITS YOU'LL GAIN

1. You'll instill confidence in your buyers. They'll be impressed by your professionalism and they'll want to buy from you.
2. You'll arrive safely and on time at your destination, because you planned it that way.
3. You won't waste time showing the wrong house.
4. You'll avoid confusion. It will be easy for the buyer to make a choice from among the few houses you carefully select.
5. You'll keep control and do the leading instead of being led.
6. You won't fumble. You'll give a smooth performance.
7. You'll be mentally alert to the buyers' reactions and you'll act accordingly.
8. You'll skillfully develop the steps to lead your prospects toward making a favorable decision.
9. You'll make each showing count.
10. You'll work smarter, not harder. You'll show fewer houses, yet sell more. You'll be showing and selling by design, not by accident.

TECHNIQUES YOU CAN USE TO GAIN THESE BENEFITS

Follow the formula—preparation plus matching property to prospect produces peak performances

In this formula, *preparation* applies to both factors—your prospect and the property. As with most formulas, when you omit one of the factors you automatically alter the results. In order to attain a peak performance, you must know and consider both the prospect and the property, not one without the other.

First, carefully qualify and counsel your prospects (as in Chapter 6), so that you will know their specifications and understand their motivations. Second, tackle the other factor of finding the right properties to show your prospects, by heeding and applying what you have learned about them. This takes a considerable amount of planning. In addition to preparing specific data, information, brochures, forms, rate books, maps, and whatever other supplies you may need, there are some important matters for you to determine: Which house will you select? Why? How many? Which route will you take? In what sequence will you show the houses?

By implementing this formula of "preparation plus matching the property to the prospect produces a peak performance," you will discover, as I have, that you can sell a house the first or second time out with your buyers.

The secret of selecting the right houses

Some salespeople run into trouble at this point when they determine which houses to show. Sometimes it's because the agent doesn't pay close enough attention to what the buyers have said or he lacks empathy and lets his own personal feelings creep into his choice of houses. Then again, some salespeople pick houses at random or show just their own listings, hoping to be able to match the prospect to the property. It is a waste of time to show houses that don't fit the buyers. They get annoyed and discouraged. And unless you happen to get lucky, you will end up frustrated and without a sale.

However, by using a professional approach by which you qualify your buyers, you will know all about them—what they need, what they really want, and what they can actually afford. Listen closely to everything they reveal about themselves. Now, as you search through the available listings, you can keep asking yourself, "Will this house satisfy their emotional needs, as well as meeting their requirements? Will it trigger their hot button and turn them on?"

With these thoughts uppermost in your mind, you can select the houses that most accurately match your buyers' wants and needs. This is the secret of choosing the right houses to show them.

Previewing can be rewarding

Previewing is time-consuming but it can be very rewarding. Even when you take time out to inspect a house you have seen before, a second look might give you a new perspective. You will view the house with your particular prospects in mind and you will see it through their eyes to determine whether or not this house could be what they are looking for.

There are some other advantages to previewing, such as a) you can determine the best route to take, b) you'll know the neighborhood, c) you will be able to show the house more effectively because you are familiar with it, and d) you can gather some useful information from the sellers about why they're selling, how motivated they are, what activity they have had, what terms and occupancy date they might be receptive to, and what particular features they enjoyed most in the house or neighborhood. This kind of information can be beneficial in producing the key to your sale, both in showing the house and later on when you're negotiating.

Arranging appointments

It is generally adequate to plan on allowing 40 minutes between appointments. This kind of spacing gives you enough time to show the prospects unhurriedly through the house and get to your next appointment on time. There may, however, be extenuating circumstances that will make you late or prevent you from keeping an appointment. In such cases, when you notify the sellers, they usually understand and appreciate the fact that you let them know. This act of common courtesy helps to maintain good rapport with the sellers, and they'll be cooperative if you should need to show the house at another time. The buyers will also be impressed.

How many houses?

The purpose of being thorough in qualifying your prospects, and then being diligent in selecting homes which you know will please them, is to make it easy for them to decide to buy that day. When you show them too many houses, they end up being fatigued, frustrated, and frightfully confused. You can avoid this by limiting the showings to three or four houses. This is usually a sufficient number from which they can comfortably make a satisfactory choice.

In what sequence?

Plan your sequence in the order which will work best for you. My preference is to save the best for last. It is a psychological approach that gradually builds up the buyers' interest. When their desire and excitement are at a peak, you are in a position to take advantage of this climax and close.

Planning the best route

There is usually more than one way to get to the homes you

have selected. It might be helpful to take a few extra minutes and plan the best way to get there or to determine the most scenic route. From your buyers' point of view, there may be some interesting landmarks to point out. You should try to avoid going through heavy traffic or poor, ugly neighborhoods. These are some of the things to consider in creating a favorable first impression of the approach to each house.

As you drive along carefully, you will have an opportunity to get better acquainted with your buyers and their children. You can learn about their hobbies, their interests, and their jobs.

Meeting your prospects

You will need to decide on the most advantageous place to meet your prospects. Meeting at the office does offer some distinct advantages. When you graciously meet and greet prospects at the office, the atmosphere sets the tone for conducting serious business. Automatically, they are in a receptive mood. You're in control, deciding when to leave and when to return. They are your captive audience so that when you return you will have a chance to complete your day's business by closing, providing additional information, or setting up the next appointment. You can comfortably brief your buyers on what is going to transpire.

Although you may be tempted to tell all about the properties you have selected, the less you say about them the better. It should be sufficient to talk in generalities, such as: "From what you have told me, I have selected some houses that I'm sure you'll like." Then continue briefly describing features, stressing those that they said were important to them: "All of the homes I have selected meet your requirements of four bedrooms, three baths, with pool and large family room. They're in choice neighborhoods and within your price range of $125,000 to $150,000. None are older than 15 years. You'll also be pleased with the spacious grounds. Each house is situated on an acre with plenty of trees, and each offers the privacy you said was important to you. I feel certain that one of these will be just what you are looking for. If so, is there anything to prevent you from making a decision today?"

Arriving at the house

If the owners are at home, present your card, and, if you wish, politely but briefly introduce your prospects. Let the owners know that you're ready to show the house. Sellers understand when you say, "Thank you, Mrs. Seller, we'll go through the house and I'll let you know when we'll be leaving." Something like this indicates that they are to make themselves scarce and that you won't be needing them for anything further.

Even if you have a key and have been led to believe that there will not be anyone at home, it is still advisable to double-check. Ring the bell and announce yourself as you enter by shouting, "Hello, anyone at home?" This will prevent any embarrassing or frightening confrontations.

As you go through the house, turn on lights, pull up shades, and draw open drapes to make the house as light and bright as possible. This will show off the house to maximum advantage, just as the jeweler did in displaying the diamond.

Permitting the joy of discovery

Even though you control the showing, direct the order of the rooms, and keep your clients together as you guide them through the house, there's still one more thing you can do. And that is to allow them the fun and excitement of discovering for themselves some of the special features each house has to offer. When you tell them only a little in advance, they won't have any preconceived notions and they won't build up any mental images of what to expect. Then they will not be disappointed. Buyers love to be surprised.

How to make the most of each showing

Here are some tried and proven ground rules you can follow to effectively show a house.

Show the house through the buyers' eyes. Accent the benefits you know will appeal to them: "You'll find this house warmer in the winter and cooler in the summer because of the insulation ... You'll appreciate all of the extra closets; there never seems to be too many, does there? ... What a beautiful view from here, isn't it?"

Slowly guide your prospects through. Let them linger in the rooms they want to study. Give them a chance to mentally move in without interrupting their thoughts with conversation. If they are unhurried, they can silently sell themselves.

Ask for their opinions. It's a good practice to try to determine the prospect's view before expounding on your own. Otherwise, you may find that you are introducing objections unnecessarily. First check to find out what they think, simply by asking, "How do you feel about air-conditioning units? ... Do you like fireplaces? ... What do you think of this house? ... " The answers may surprise you. What is pleasing and desirable for one person may be totally objectionable to another. You'll be safe if you never assume anything, but instead find out.

Suggest a second look. After you have toured the house, an effective technique you can use is to suggest that the prospects take a second look. "Mr. and Mrs. Buyer, wouldn't you like to go through again on your own? It's usually pretty difficult to see everything the first time, isn't it? Perhaps there are some things you'd like to check. Take your time, and when you're finished I'll be glad to answer any other questions you may have."

This is a great way to find out where you stand in the sale. If they say, "No, thank you, we've seen everything we need to," you can be quite certain that they're not interested in the house. If, however, they do go back, that's an indication that they are considering it. Of course, "We really like it" means, "We're ready to buy," and you should proceed to write up the offer without further ado. More questions mean, "We're thinking about it ... We're not quite sure." They may need some reassurance.

If you haven't been asking your prospects to take a second look, try it. You may be pleasantly surprised, as was one of the students in a course I gave on "The Art of Selling Real Estate."

Matilda told the class that she and her husband had decided to test the market. One Sunday, they put out a "For Sale" sign. A few couples came by. To one couple, she suggested that they go through the house once again. Sure enough, when they returned they said that they liked the house and wanted to buy it. Matilda laughingly told us that they were caught by surprise, because they hadn't been prepared to sell it that day.

You'll find that going back for another look works well when your prospects seem to be wavering, fearful of making a final decision: "You seem to have some doubts. I know this is a big decision to make and you want to make sure, don't you? So, let's go back and take another look. Then you'll feel better about whatever you decide." Offering to go back again usually reassures them.

Focus on their "hot buttons." When you selected the houses to show your customers, you concentrated on choosing those houses that you knew would motivate them. Keeping these emotional needs in mind and being aware of the fact that people buy with their hearts rather than with their heads, you should call attention to those needs: "In addition to all the fine features this house offers, look at these magnificent grounds! Just what you said you wanted—an interesting assortment of trees on an impressive acre, and what privacy! Isn't it great?"

Listen for their reactions. Encourage the buyers to do the talking. This gives you a golden opportunity to listen. By doing so you also avoid a deadly temptation for many real estate salespeople, that of telling all they know. When you listen you can pay close attention to what your prospects say and observe their movements and facial expressions. Since these indicate their reactions, both good and bad, you can guide yourself accordingly. Chapter 4 tells you how to listen effectively.

Some salespeople take each objection or complaint seriously. As a result they feel compelled to go into lengthy discussion to try to overcome each and every one. Instead of doing this, you should initially try to disregard an objection. If it is repeated again and again, you can deal with it then.

In the event that you encounter too many serious objections, it would be best to forget the house and go on to the next one.

Heed buying signals. When your customers do or say anything to indicate that they see themselves living in that house, they are sending out a message: "We're ready, we want to buy." These signals might consist of figuring out how to handle the financial end, deciding where they could place the furniture, choosing bedrooms for the children, whispering among themselves, or asking questions such as, "Do you think the seller is firm on his price?" or, "If we should decide on this house, when would we be able to move in?" Another favorable indicator is when they answer "yes" to all your questions. They might also give you the signal simply by saying that they like something. The expert salesperson takes advantage of any and all buying signals. He stops talking and finalizes the sale.

The tip-off clue

The most powerful closing technique I know of is to ask, "What do you think of it?" and then pause and wait for the complete answer. The technique also applies to showing a house. At the end of the tour, if you ask, "What do you think of this house" and then listen to the response, your prospects will reveal their feelings—their interest or indifference, their objections, concerns, or desires.

As you finish showing each house, repeat the same question: "What do you think of this house?" Then, after you have heard all that they have to say, ask the next question: *"How do you think this house compares with the previous house?"* or "with the second or third house?" Once again, hear them out without interruption. It takes practice to refrain from talking before the other people have said everything they have on their minds.

Buyers welcome this opportunity to air their thoughts after each viewing, but most importantly, what they say gives you the clues you need to consummate the sale.

The last step

If your buyers have indicated interest, then it is just a matter of winding things up. However, if for some reason you cannot complete the sale, set up a definite time and date for the next appointment before leaving your prospects. The purpose of the new appointment could be to furnish additional information or to go out again as soon as possible. Once the prospects leave you, all kinds of things can happen. They can go off on their own, go out with another agent, or completely discard any further thought of what you showed them. So, making definite arrangements works out well for everyone. You know for sure what you have to do and when. The prospects feel committed, yet they are relieved to know that you are devoting yourself to helping them.

How to make open houses count

Some salespeople look upon open houses primarily as a duty they perform to placate the sellers. However, those agents who treat open houses as an opportunity for things to happen often find that they do. You can end up selling that house and getting some good prospects for other sales and listings.

To make each open house pay off, start with a well-worded ad to attract potential buyers. Then tell everyone about the time and date. Invite the neighbors. They're usually curious anyway. They may have friends or relatives whom they would like to have living near them. They may also be thinking of selling their house and will welcome a chance to ask you some questions. When you talk to your associates, let them know about your open house. They like the convenience of dropping in without arranging to pick up keys or setting up a definite time. Your house could be the very house for their prospects. Of course, you should also invite your own prospects to drop in.

A salesman I knew had been working unsuccessfully with a particular prospect. Although he didn't think that this would be the right house, he suggested that they come to an open house on Sunday afternoon. Very much to the salesman's surprise, his prospects bought that house. Interestingly enough, they happened to be the only ones who showed up that day.

In addition to announcing the open house, there are a few more preparations to make. These include pulling up shades, opening drapes, putting on soft background music, and turning on necessary lights to brighten up the house. Check to make sure that you have on hand any supplies you may need such as your cards, brochures, contract forms, rate book, a guest list or book, scratch pad, and pens. At an open house, you don't have the opportunity to pre-qualify the callers, so a guest book or sheet is very helpful. As people arrive you can ask them to please sign in, saying that your office likes to keep records of the results of open houses. The guest book would have them list their name, address, phone number, and whether they came because they saw the ad or the sign. This information can be most beneficial, especially if you get busy and don't have time to complete conversations with some of the viewers. You can contact them later.

As for the sellers, they probably won't be around because when you made arrangements for the open house you explained that they should be absent or inconspicuous so that they could leave the showing and selling to you.

As you guide people through the house, you should casually ask some qualifying questions about how soon they need a house, what they are looking for, how long they have been looking, whether they are looking for themselves or for someone else, and what they think of this house. This information can reveal if they are good prospects for this house or any other, or if they're just "Sunday lookers."

After you have held a house open, your seller expects and appreciates two things: 1) that the house is left as you found it, with doors locked, lights and music off, and curtains, drapes, and windows closed, and 2) a brief report of the day's activity. Doing these two things helps to keep your seller satisfied with your service.

Key review points to ponder

Although particular techniques for successfully showing houses have been discussed in this chapter, there's still more involved in selling a house. The various selling situations include specific selling techniques, which are discussed elsewhere in the individual chapters covering preparation, qualifying the buyer, asking questions, listening, negotiating, and closing.

However, to sum up this chapter, here are some of the do's and don'ts to remember, so that you can show and sell a house by design, rather than by accident:

- Do plenty of homework.
- Feel confident that you will sell today.
- Carefully counsel and qualify your customers.
- Put yourself in the other person's shoes.
- Select only properties that match the prospects.
- Don't waste time showing the wrong houses.
- Give a warm, friendly greeting at the office.
- Say little in advance about the houses.
- Advise the sellers to be absent at the time of the showing.
- Pick the prettiest route to get to the house.
- Drive carefully.
- Be punctual.
- Show only three or four houses, 40 minutes apart.
- Show the best house last.
- Turn on lights and music, and open shades.
- Don't assume—ask questions.
- Don't offer opinions—let your prospects tell you theirs.
- Don't talk too much—listen instead.
- Linger in the room they like best.
- Watch for reactions and buying signals.
- Ask, "What do you think about this house?"

- **Try closing often.**
- **Don't leave without a signed contract or a definite next appointment.**

In the end, you'll show fewer houses and sell more.

Checklist for Showing Property Effectively

Do you ask the buyers enough probing questions?

    Find out their real reasons for buying?

    Know the specific features they require?

    Uncover and understand which benefits are most important to them?

Do you use a computer-type method in choosing the properties to match both their needs and their wants?

Do you preview the house?

    Find out the sellers' reasons for selling, degree of motivation, desired occupancy date, favorite house features?

Do you select the best viewing order?

Do you avoid confusing the buyers by showing them too many houses (more than three or four)?

Do you travel along a route that whets their appetite?

    Use interim time to get better acquainted, instill confidence and trust in your ability to help them?

Do you get off to a good start?

    Meet the prospects at the office?

    Refrain from divulging particulars about the houses?

Do you follow fundamental rules for effective showings by:

    Precluding any interference from the sellers?

    Selecting the most effective order of showing the rooms?

    Permitting the buyers the joy of discovering for themselves?

    Letting the buyers feel unhurried?

    Encouraging them to express their honest reactions?

Do you determine the extent or lack of interest after the first tour?

    Suggest that they take a second look through the house?

    After each showing, ask the important closing question, "What do you think of this house?"

Attempt to get the buyers back for still another look when they are deliberating?

Pay close attention to their answers?

Do you leave with a definite next appointment if you were not successful in closing?

Do you see good results from the open house?

Arrange to contact the promising prospects for buying or selling?

Do you review the key points for selling by design?

13

Failure to

Use the Real Estate Salesperson's

Most Effective Clincher

Everyone loves a story. Children are delighted when you say, "I'll tell you a story." Adults never really outgrow the pleasure of listening to stories, as is evidenced by the popularity of novels, movies, and plays. How many thousands are addicted to TV soap operas?

Master salespeople recognize this and utilize the magical influence that storytelling has on people. The greatest preachers, all super salespeople, also do most of their "selling" with stories. This is because they know that the world's greatest closer of sales is a story. Yet, surprisingly, many real estate agents, if questioned, would have to admit that they have not consciously developed this most powerful and motivating method of selling.

Sometime ago, I learned from books written by master salesmen, such as Frank Bettger, Charles B. Roth, and Edwin Charles Greif, that a story is a wonderful way to make a particular point or get an idea across. That is why you'll find so many stories specified throughout this book. As you read the actual examples, they will help you to understand and accept the idea a little better. And, in those cases where you have had a similar experience, you will nod your head and say to yourself, "How true! Yes, I see the point you're making."

That's how a buyer or seller reacts when you tell him a story. They, too, are interested in hearing about true cases that dramatize how someone else handles a similar situation.

THE BENEFITS YOU'LL GAIN

1. You'll quickly win your prospect's attention and interest.
2. You'll gain courage and confidence in your selling ability.
3. You'll get your point or idea across in an indirect manner. Your selling will be low-key.
4. Your buyer or seller will sell himself. He'll identify himself with the character in the story.
5. You'll overcome objections by dramatizing how someone else gained or lost, removing doubts, and preventing procrastination.
6. You'll save your buyers and sellers from possible disappointments.
7. Your direct testimonials from previous customers in similar situations will be credible endorsements of what you are telling your buyers. This third-party story will influence them.
8. Narratives will be effective in any selling situation.
9. Storytelling will accomplish some valuable goals. It will:
   a) Serve as an example to demonstrate a point or an idea.
   b) Relieve tension.
   c) Stimulate decision.
   d) Revive the sale.
   e) Rescue the sale.
   f) Clinch the sale.
10. Using interesting and appropriate stories will have overwhelming weight in listing more properties, closing more sales, and making you a more successful real estate salesperson.

TECHNIQUES YOU CAN USE TO GAIN THESE BENEFITS

Guidelines for storytelling

Although everyone loves a story, not all stories are appropriate or interesting to your customers and clients. This, of course, eliminates jokes and stories that merely entertain.

Rule number one, then, is to tell a story that fits your buyers and sellers. This means that the story must relate to a problem that is facing them. When you tell them about someone else who had a similar experience, you arouse their interest and they will listen intently to learn the outcome. Because they identify with the character of the story, they may decide to solve their own problem in the same way.

Rule number two is that, in order to be effective, your story must be interesting and well-told. Unless your prospect can see himself as the central figure, he'll lose interest. However, once you succeed in arousing his interest, he will feel involved and, in the process, he may sell himself.

To make a story interesting, you must be enthusiastic, build suspense, and make the action seem natural. No matter how many times you repeat the same story, if you can tell it as though it were the first time, your listener will become enthralled, lean forward a bit, savor each word, and finally perform exactly as you intended him to.

Rule three states that, to be effective, the story should be to the point. If you ramble on, introducing irrelevant matters, you'll lose your prospects' interest and their business. But, if you stick to the pertinent details about features, facts, people, and places, you will make the story interesting and credible.

Rule four is the most important. In order for a story to be acceptable and influential, all of the details must be correct. Otherwise, your story will fail. You will run the risk of having your prospect disregard the story and discard you, because he will not believe anything else you tell him.

A story any time

Your entire presentation can include a series of stories— stories about satisfied sellers, stories about sad sellers who over-priced their properties, stories about quick sales, happy buyers, or disappointed buyers. The list goes on and on. There's no end to the stories you can use to show how someone else gained satisfaction or lamented a loss. For instance, here's a simple story I use whenever it seems advisable to use a lock box but the seller is reluctant to do so.

To introduce the story, I start by asking the sellers if they have ever seen a lock box, and then I demonstrate how it works, thus focusing their attention on an exhibit. "Because we want to have the house sold as quickly as possible, we don't want to overlook any opportunity. From experience, we have found that this little lock box can be a very valuable tool."

Then comes the story: "The sellers had moved out on Thursday from their lovely four bedroom home with a pool in Mangowood, and on Friday the lock box was installed. In the late afternoon of the next day, a saleswoman was combing that particular area with a wealthy out-of-town family, who were there to buy a house that weekend. The saleswoman spotted the lock box, used the key to show them the house, and they liked it. She immediately contacted me and an appointment was quickly arranged to present the contract to the sellers, who had already moved a few miles away. Finally, the contract was accepted and the house was sold.

"The interesting part of this story is that, if there had not been a lock box on the house and the saleswoman had waited until the next day to get a key to show them the house, there would have been no sale.

"The day before, the buyers had seen a house that they liked better. They had made an offer on it which was rejected. The very next morning, which was after they had purchased my listing, the previous seller called the saleswoman to say that he had changed his mind and was now willing to accept the buyers' offer. Of course, it was too late. That little lock box had saved the sale for my seller!

"Mr. and Mrs. Seller, this is the sort of thing that happens. You see, don't you, what a convenient and helpful selling tool this lock box is?"

It is natural for the sellers to visualize a similar situation happening to them. They invariably agree to use the lock box.

When all else fails, tell a story

When you've tried several closing techniques and the buyers still insist that they want to think it over, don't despair. There is still another tactic to use. Tell a story, a true one about someone who felt exactly as they did, using specific details that are appropriate and with which they can identify. The story may be about someone they know, or a house or street that is familiar. You might show them a brochure or other evidence of the house you are telling them about. The details make the story interesting and credible, even if your prospect doesn't know the house or the people involved. Then, when you end the story with the convincing solution, they will see the solution as the answer to their problem, too. The story does it. It overcomes their hesitancy and sells them. It is a very powerful technique.

Feel, Felt, and Found are the key words: "I understand how you *feel*, Mr. and Mrs. Buyer. Let me tell you about Mr. and Mrs. O., a very nice couple about your age who *felt* the way you do. They didn't want to rush into anything. They decided to think it over during the weekend. Bright and early on Monday morning, they came to my office to say that they had given the matter serious thought and had decided to buy the house. Guess what? They *found* out that another salesman had shown the house during the weekend and had sold it. As you can imagine, Mr. and Mrs. O. were heartbroken. They had really wanted that house. Although they started looking again, they never did find another house that they liked as well. I wouldn't want that to happen to you, Mr. and Mrs. Buyer. Don't let the chance slip away."

Buyers and sellers alike relate and respond to such stories that include the key words *feel, felt,* and *found.* They see themselves as the central figures of the narrative and are very interested. They feel involved. They find themselves swayed and convinced.

This kind of story actually acts as a third party to influence your prospects in any selling situation, whether you are listing, selling property, or negotiating. Try using this technique when a seller balks at accepting a fair market price, when a buyer is reluctant to make an offer with an adequate earnest money deposit, or whenever your sale is running into trouble. When you do, you'll discover that this method of storytelling is undeniably powerful in doing two things—rescuing your sale *and* closing it.

Bring on the witnesses

A truly professional salesman gives the impression that he's not selling. He lets the stories do the selling for him. This is an indirect method of selling that does a super job of convincing. People like this because, as you know, no one likes to feel that he is being pressured, coerced, or sold. A prospect resents that. He wants to feel that he is making up his own mind.

Another effective yet easy way to use the third-party influence is to follow a story with a testimonial letter from a satisfied customer or client. Not only does this reinforce what you have said, but it greatly influences your prospect, especially if the person you are selling is a stranger. You're letting them see for themselves what someone else said about what was done to satisfy them.

You can also use printed material as a witness. This could include such things as compiled facts, newspaper clippings, and brochures. The written word further attests to the point of your story.

Always a story

Take a look at some of the wonderful ways you can use this versatile and successful technique. Your story can:

- Answer a question: "I can best explain with a story ... "
- Overcome an objection: "I understand. Here's a situation I'd like to share with you ... "
- Retrieve a sale: "Here's something I think will interest you ... "
- Revive a sale: "When I heard this story, it reminded me of your predicament ... "
- Close a sale: "Would you like to hear how ... "

No matter what the difficulty is, you can always handle it with a story. It is one of the most powerful selling and closing weapons.

Remember the criteria of a good story: It must be interesting, true, and appropriate to the situation and the person you are selling. Feel free to use any of the stories in this book, although you must have similar stories of your own that you can use as well. Whether the story is your own or someone else's doesn't matter. The important thing is for you to become a good storyteller. When you do, you'll close more sales and enjoy added income.

Checklist for Using the Real Estate Salesperson's Most Effective Clincher

Do you choose appropriate stories to tell which relate to your prospects' problems and situations?

Feel that you hold the prospects' attention?

Refrain from rambling on?

Tell only true stories, with totally correct details?

Use stories to reinforce positive statements?

Include visual items for demonstration purposes?

Use a story as a last resort closing tool?

Include a situation with which your buyer or seller can empathize, using the words *feel, felt,* and *found*?

Liberally use stories to do the selling for you?

Use a story to: answer a question? overcome an objection? retrieve the sale? revive the sale? finally close the sale?

14

Failure to
Get Offers Accepted Quickly

"Wish me luck! I'll do my very best for you." These are your parting words to your buyers as you take off to tackle a tough and most crucial selling job: closing the seller.

Up to this point you have been proficient and professional. From your careful qualifying, you know that you have a bona fide buyer, one who is ready, willing, and able to buy this house. They've committed themselves in writing with an earnest money deposit. But, as you know, until there is a meeting of the minds of both the buyer and the seller, you don't have a sale, and all you have done so far could go down the drain.

That is precisely why the successful real estate salesperson takes the trouble to protect himself. He knows that, by skillfully selling the seller, he insures the time and energy he has invested.

THE BENEFITS YOU'LL GAIN

1. You'll control the discussions. You won't be intimidated by others, by the buyer, the seller, the listing agent, or the attorney.
2. The other parties will respect your expertise and they'll cooperate.
3. You'll be prepared for any contingencies that may arise.

4. Your positive attitude will permeate the discussions and influence those involved.

5. You'll invite discussion, not confrontation, with your calm, professional manner.

6. Your commission will be assured.

7. You'll successfully complete the transaction and be free to move on to others.

8. You'll close more sales more quickly, which spells *success.*

Yet, despite these advantages, many salespeople spin their wheels, spend endless hours showing buyers around, and finally succeed in obtaining an offer, only to get shot down at the negotiating table.

TECHNIQUES YOU CAN USE TO GAIN THESE BENEFITS

How to call for an appointment

Strike while the iron is hot. Since there is always the possibility that another agent might introduce an offer ahead of yours, or the buyers might withdraw their offer, play it safe. Contact the sellers as soon as possible—*never* delay presenting any offer.

When a successful closer calls for an appointment to present his offer, he knows from experience that he's interested in only one thing: setting up a time and place to meet. He never permits himself to get drawn into a discussion on the phone. All he wants is the appointment, the opportunity to effectively present his offer in person, so that he can obtain confirmation in writing.

Preventing leaks

You may wonder what harm there is in letting anyone know in advance the contents of your offer. For one thing, divulging the price alone can prove devastating to your sale. If the seller knows the price beforehand, he may reject the offer completely based on price alone, and may never learn about the terms, which could be of equal importance to him. But, an even greater danger is that you sacrifice the chance of presenting your entire offer in a psychologically effective fashion that encourages the seller to engage in discussion and negotiation that can ultimately be beneficial to all parties. If, furthermore, the listing agent knows the price, he may decide incorrectly for the seller and discourage you from submitting your offer, or he may influence the seller's thinking before you have had the opportunity to present your offer in total; or, he may even encourage one of his own buyers to increase their offer slightly above yours. Since you never know for sure who is working on what, any information regarding your offer could be beneficial to other associates in your office or the listing office. Any one of them might be working with buyers who are interested in making an offer on the same property.

Therefore, in all fairness to your buyer, the seller, and yourself, the details of the contract should remain confidential until you meet face-to-face with the sellers.

How to handle phoning the seller

Every owner is eager to know the price of the offer. A simple way to avoid giving him this information is to have someone else make the phone call, perhaps the office secretary or an associate. Then, when the seller asks any questions, the person making the call can honestly say that he doesn't know.

This protects you from getting involved in an awkward conversation: "Hello, Mrs. Seller, I'm calling for John Smith. He has an offer on your house and would like to present it this evening. Will 6:30 be a convenient time for you and Mr. Seller?"

Or, if *you* have to make the call: "Mrs. Seller, I'm working with Mr. and Mrs. Buyer. We're drawing up a contract on your house. The details are not complete yet, but I want to make sure that both you and Mr. Seller will be at home this evening. Would 6:30 be a convenient time to come by?"

The sale before the sale

With an offer in hand, you're tempted to rush right over to present it, hoping that you can convince the seller to take it. But, with just a few minutes for planning and preparation, you could put your sale "in the bag." Here's how:

1. Prepare the folder file you are taking with you. Include a copy of the listing agreement, the brochure, comparables, ads, the record of activity, offers to date, any facts you feel will be persuasive.

2. Memorize the key points of the deposit receipt.

3. Think of all possible reasons why the seller might reject the offer. How will you handle each one if any of them should arise? What

do you know about why he is selling? What answers can you give to show him that now he can have his problem solved?

4. Decide on a few reserve selling points to use as clinchers, such as concessions that the buyer might make as a trade-off for something that the seller objects to. This could be something like not including the washer and dryer to adjust the price, a second mortgage to take up the difference in price, a change of terms regarding occupancy, inspections of the roof, termites, or pool.

When you are prepared for whatever contingency might arise, you can go forth with confidence and courage in order to be convincing.

Upon arrival

After a brief initial greeting and introductions, you can indicate that you intend to conduct the presentation of your offer in a professional manner: "Mr. Seller, may we please sit at a table where it will be convenient to show you the information I have?" This simple act puts everyone in a respectful and responsive mood.

Directing the seating

As you head toward the table, direct the sellers to sit opposite you. When you do this, you can easily observe how they react without moving your head from side to side. And they won't be able to signal each other without you seeing them.

The stage is thus set, you've taken charge, you have their undivided attention, and everyone is waiting eagerly for you to continue.

How to disclose the contents of the contract

If you just hand the sellers a copy of the contract for them to read, they'll probably stop at the word *price* and read no further. On the other hand, a lengthy introduction would be quite ineffective because, while you're talking, they're only half listening. All this time, they are thinking about the offer, waiting and wondering how much it is. You should save whatever you have to say about the buyers or the difficulties you encountered for a later time when you can use such information effectively if you meet resistance.

Start the proceedings by using a psychological approach. Leave the folder file closed on the table and begin closing the sellers by obtaining commitments on those key points of the contract that you memorized, such as amount of deposit, closing date, and personal property items.

"I have here a check from Mr. and Mrs. Buyer for $1000 as their initial deposit for the purchase of your home. Within 24 hours of your acceptance, they will increase the deposit to a full 10 percent of the purchase price. This meets with your approval, doesn't it?

"The Buyers like the drapes and carpeting and have included them. Is that all right with you?

"Mr. Seller, like you, Mr. Buyer likes to do his own repairs around the house, so they have included the workbench in the garage. That's okay, isn't it?

"And you'll be pleased to know that they would like to be in the house by the first of October or sooner. That fits right in with your plans, doesn't it?"

From a series of questions such as these, you can see how easy it is for you to obtain "yes" answers. This method conditions the sellers' minds. They are now visualizing their house as sold. Since they are in a receptive state of mind, it is easier for you to get approval on the major items. This is the same technique you used successfully when you obtained the offer from the buyers. Then, you also closed on minor points first.

Controlling your speech muscles

After these oral commitments, pass out a copy of the contract to each person present, with the deposit check attached to Mr. Seller's copy. Then, silently sit by, permitting the sellers to read the contract uninterrupted. The wait will seem endless, but you'll discover that this period of silence is enormously important. When they are finished, you'll know from their questions, comments, and the tones of their voices what they are thinking. These are the clues to guide you in determining what you should say or do to conclude the transaction satisfactorily.

A word of caution

If the listing agent interrupts the reading, politely but firmly say something like, "John, let's give Mr. and Mrs. Seller a chance to finish reading the contract. Then let's hear what they have to say, or if they have any questions they'd like answered." This indicates to the lister that he sould be courteous and allow the sellers to speak for themselves.

When the seller says, "No! This won't do!"

To the angry "No, we can't accept this," or, "I could have saved you the trouble of coming here if you had given us this information on the phone," try this response:

In a low, calm, and collected voice, say, "Mr. Seller, I understand your disappointment, but by state law we are required to submit all offers to the sellers. However, you do have three options: 1) you can reject it, 2) you can accept it, or 3) we can do something to keep it alive.

"The Buyers want to buy your house. They are ready, willing, and qualified to do so. So, let's see what we can do to make this contract acceptable to you."

Let's collaborate

Let's, a cooperative word, means "you and I together." It is much more effective than saying, "This is a good offer. I think you should consider it." The idea is the same, but when you say "let's," it's much more acceptable to the other person. He doesn't feel he is being coerced. He realizes that you're working for and with him as in any partnership.

I have found that the word *let's* is extremely helpful in any closing situation, especially when negotiating. I have often been surprised by some of the ideas a buyer or seller has come up with. They have been the ones to really clinch the sale.

Asking, "What do you think?"—a good way to find out

What better way is there to get your seller's reaction than to simply ask him? Without any hesitation, he'll gladly tell you. And, if you carry it one step further and ask him what he likes and doesn't like about the contract, you'll gain a better insight into his thinking. By listening closely, you can usually detect what is most important to him at the time. This could be quite different from his original thinking when the listing was signed.

There are two more advantages of asking for their reactions: 1) you won't assume anything, you'll know, and 2) you won't be tempted to offer opinions which could be opposite to those of the sellers and could cause conflict and confusion.

The magic of "What if?"

"What if" is a wonderful phrase to use when your buyer or seller is considering a counteroffer. "*What if* I can get the price to $75,000? ... *What if* I can get them to agree on a later occupancy? ... *What if* I can get them to split the cost of the roof repairs? ... *What if* I can get them to do whatever you're asking? ... I don't know if I can do it, but if I can, will the contract then be acceptable to you?"

In addition to alerting your clients that you anticipate some resistance from the other party, you are also putting them on notice that if you should succeed in meeting these demands there will be no doubt that the transaction will be final. This prevents them from entertaining any thoughts about making more changes later on. The next time you find yourself caught between seller and buyer, try this simple technique.

$500 apart

As an example, let's say that your seller purchased his house for $35,000, and listed it 10 years later for sale at $55,000. The final offer is for $54,500, and he's about to reject it. Try this approach:

"Mr. Seller, suppose you were in Monte Carlo at the Casino, had a fine dinner, spent the evening shooting craps at the dice table, and amassed a pile of $54,500. But you're not yet satisfied; you're determined to make it $55,000. Your wife says, "Come on, let's quit and go home." Would you push it all back to try to win that extra $500, or would you take your money and leave?"

When you personalize the situation by using figures that apply to the sale of his house, the seller realizes that he is doing just that—he's gambling.

As you can see, this is a most effective technique to use when you have succeeded in narrowing the difference down to around $500 or $1000.

Presenting counteroffers

Just as you carefully planned your presentation of the original offer, it is also advisable to prepare your thoughts about how you can effectively present the counteroffer. This time, however, it is how and what you say as an introduction that makes a difference.

If you rush right in and happily announce your success, even if it's exactly what the buyers wanted, they'll think it was too easy.

They'll wonder if they've overlooked something, or if they could do even better. However, if before you tell them anything specific, you dramatize the difficult time you had, things will be quite different. Tell them about how the sellers refused to concede on a certain item, tell them how at one point the sellers decided not to make any counteroffer at all, tell them how hard you had to work to obtain this counteroffer. When you share your endeavors honestly with them, they will appreciate how much time and effort you put forth in their behalf. Consequently, they are inclined to look at the counteroffer you have brought them much more favorably.

Camp David meeting—a good example

The historic signing of the documents after the Camp David meeting between Prime Minister Begin, President Sadat, and President Carter was a classical example of greatly dramatizing the events leading up to an agreement. Before disclosing the specifics of the documents, President Carter explained that they were a framework for a peace treaty. Then, each of the three men described the difficulties, the problems, the long hours of hard work, and the frustrations of those 13 days at Camp David. They also said that each knew how much was at stake, but that there were times when any agreement seemed impossible. Even near the end, failure appeared to be inevitable.

While they shared all of this, the whole world listened attentively and marvelled at their final success. This was, indeed, a superb selling job in getting their accomplishments favorably accepted by everyone, including the press and the people of the United States and other countries.

How to handle "We'd like to think it over"

You might say, "Yes, by all means I agree that you should think it over. I'll just go into the next room and give you a chance to discuss it in privacy," or, "I'll go out for a cup of coffee," or, "I'll go to the office; there are some papers I need to pick up." Whatever you offer to do gives your clients an opportunity to be alone and discuss the matter privately. This is usually all they need to convince each other.

Afterwards, if they are still procrastinating, convince them of the importance of weighing the benefits of a decision against the uncertainties of indecision.

The perils of indecision

"Mr. and Mrs. Seller, if you sign this contract right now, you will have your house sold and you can go about making definite plans for moving. But, if there are some changes you'd like to make to keep this contract alive, let's start putting them down. If you delay too long, we may lose the buyers. We know from experience that buyers often get fearful, or in the meantime they may find something else that they like better. The Buyers could change their minds, and they do have the right to withdraw their offer. Sellers don't usually realize that this could happen until it is too late. That's just what happened to the Jones's." Then you could relate an appropriate true story.

Leaving with something specific

No matter how long it takes, the star salesperson makes it a point to leave the seller with either a signed contract or a counteroffer. You might ask them why they are experiencing indecision, what other reasons they have, or what conditions might change tomorrow or later.

It may take perseverance and some probing, as well as drawing on the various closing techniques, to get the desired results, but in the end it will be worth the effort to save the sale.

Reporting the counteroffer

If you had promised your clients that you'd let them know as soon as you had something to report, it is most advantageous to visit them in person. However, if you feel that a call is in order, call to let them know that you're on your way. Even though you have good rapport with your clients and you feel that it's safe to tell them about the changes over the phone, it is usually a mistake to do so and can be fatal to your sale. So, no matter what the hour or the distance, it pays to present the counteroffer in person: "Mrs. Client, there are just a few brief changes I'd like to go over with you and Mr. Client before finalizing the contract. I can be there in half an hour; is that O.K. with you?"

Cooperating with the selling agent

Have you ever had the experience of presenting a fair, workable offer only to find the listing agent putting stumbling blocks in your way? You wonder why anyone would take an opposing side and try to kill a sale, when cooperation is the name of the game. There are probably two reasons for this behavior. The first is that, as the listing agent, he may be selfish and greedy. He would prefer to keep the listing, hoping to sell it himself rather than share the commission. The second reason is that the agent may become overprotective and feel that he should act as an advocate. He takes over and makes decisions for the seller about what he should or should not accept, and in the end he kills the sale. This is a great disservice to the seller, the person he represents.

This attitude is costly to everyone—the seller, the selling agent, and the lister himself. The listing might expire, or the owner may have to make greater concessions later on. Meanwhile, he may be sacrificing the opportunity to get his house sold and his problems solved now. The selling agent, of course, earns nothing for the time and effort he expends. If he doesn't lose the buyers, he must start all over again.

Acting in the spirit of cooperation, rather than opposition, is the best way to serve your seller. You'll be helping to save the sale, not sabotage it.

Two tips

If there is more than one party involved, it would be a mistake to present your offer or counteroffer to only one of the parties. Even though that person insists that he or she is the one who makes all the decisions in their family, you'll discover that it doesn't always work that way. So, to prevent problems, save what you have to show them until you can meet with both of them in person.

What should you do when you present an offer or counteroffer, and one spouse turns to the other and says, "What do you think, dear?" You should recognize this as a definite clue. The person who asks is ready to accept the offer. Sit back and let the two of them talk it out. If, however, you sense a reluctance to discuss the matter in front of you, give them space. Excuse yourself. Go into another room or suggest that they do. They will welcome the privacy for discussion and will usually arrive at a favorable conclusion. (It is interesting to note that it is the man who generally makes the decision to sell, but the woman usually decides to buy.)

The final step

After the contract has been signed and all changes have been initialed by both sellers and buyers, the last thing to do is to congratulate them enthusiastically: "Mr. and Mrs. Seller, congratulations! I'm happy for you that your house is sold. No more showings, no further worries, you can now go about making your future plans. Isn't that great?"

"Mr. and Mrs. Buyer, congratulations! You made a fine choice, and I want to wish you every happiness in your new home."

Checklist for Getting Offers Accepted Quickly

Do you avoid any delays in presenting the offer to the seller in person?

   Immediately arrange an appointment to present the offer?

   Refrain from disclosing details of the offer with the seller on the telephone, and until you see him in person?

Do you avoid discussing the offer with anyone prior to presenting it to the seller?

Do you plan and prepare to be convincing by:

   Taking the file and all material relating to the listing with you?

   Committing to memory key points of the offer?

   Anticipating answers that will handle all possible objections?

   Planning on a few "reserves" to use as compromises?

Do you take charge at the negotiating table by:

   Arranging the most advantageous seating?

   Gaining agreement on key points of the contract before revealing the price?

   Allowing all parties present to read the contract uninterrupted?

   Guiding the course of the procedure according to the seller's reaction?

Do you let the seller be the judge by:

   Asking, "What do you think of it?"

   Using "What if?" to finalize a positive commitment?

Do you use the Monte Carlo story to effectively close when one party is holding off because of a difference of a few thousand dollars?

Do you find that you convert "We'd like to think it over" into a closing opportunity?

    Provide time for the clients to think it over in a controlled, limited setting?

Do you avoid permitting procrastination?

    Help the seller arrive at some decision?

    Remain determined to leave with some contract changes, rather than nothing at all?

Do you refrain from discussing the counteroffer on the telephone?

    Politely insist on revealing the details only when you are with them face-to-face?

Do you have a helpful, courteous, and cooperative attitude toward the selling agent?

Do you refrain from presenting the offer to only one of two parties involved?

Do you avoid missing any closing clues?

Do you congratulate and compliment both buyer and seller for their wise decisions?

15

Not

Following Through

All the Way

Steven, an agent, had some out-of-town buyers who were interested in looking at $100,000 homes in a particular area. Steven called me to inquire about one particular listing which he thought would suit their needs. Not being familiar with the area or how to get there, he asked if I would accompany him.

His prospects loved everything—the location, the schools, proximity to shopping areas. The unique pool and oversized recreation area were very appealing to them. The bedroom arrangement was perfect for them and their children. They talked about which children would have which rooms and began to mentally place their furniture in the rest of the house. All of the "buy" signals were flashing loud and clear.

As we parted, the husband shook our hands, saying, "We'll be seeing you soon, we are buying the house!" Then I waited to hear from Steve. I waited and waited, but he didn't say a word. Later, I called him and asked, "What happened?" "Nothing," he replied. "They said they wanted to think it over. That's the way it was left."

This may sound unbelievable, but it is true. Steve did not invite them to his office to find out what they wanted to think over, nor did he make any attempt to follow through later. In fact, he didn't even know where and when to reach them. He just waited for them to call him.

Steve's story is just one example of how a real estate salesperson can lose thousands of dollars in commissions simply by neglecting to follow through with promising prospects.

THE BENEFITS YOU'LL GAIN

1. You'll make the most of the prospects you contact who have promising potential.
2. You'll improve the image of a professional real estate salesperson. You'll help to decrease the common complaint about agents who fail to keep buyers and sellers informed about their transactions.
3. You'll complete the business, without paving the way for someone else.
4. You'll keep buyers and sellers posted. They won't wonder and worry.
5. Your clients and customers will become satisfied sellers and blissful buyers.
6. Your clients will help you build a solid referral business and you'll have a constant supply of prospects.
7. You'll improve the ratio between your productivity and the time you spend selling.
8. You'll prevent problems and surprises at closings.
9. Finally, when you follow through, you'll generate more listings and sales, which in turn will produce greater earnings for you.

TECHNIQUES YOU CAN USE TO GAIN THESE BENEFITS

Giving up too soon makes it easy for the next salesperson

All too often, an agent works hard, does all of the groundwork, and then abandons his prospect just when the prospect is about to perform. At that point, another agent steps in and makes an easy sale.

For instance, it is a common occurrence for a salesperson to go on a listing interview, make a very good impression, and do a good job of selling the seller on the merits of using a Realtor. The only hitch is that Mr. Homeowner may not be quite ready. He may want to try it on his own for a little longer. However, this salesperson neglects to keep in close contact by making frequent call-backs, or, because he feels he has excellent rapport, he waits for the seller to call him. Since the salesperson has convinced the seller to use a Realtor, the seller decides to do just that after a few weeks. Now that he's ready to go ahead, he hands the listing to the agent who happens to be there at that moment, not to the one who spent the time, did all the work, and then disappeared.

Frequently, when showing properties, an agent may take a promising prospect out, drive him around, but then give up too soon. Mary, a broker who is a friend of mine, remarked recently how surprised she was to find so many salespeople who abandon their good prospects. They make an initial effort, but don't bother to follow through. Apropos of this, she told me about her most recent sale.

It seems that Mrs. B. had seen a house she liked very much and wanted her husband to see it. Even though she had expressed interest when she viewed the house, she had not heard again from the person who had shown it to her, and she couldn't remember the name of that salesperson. She asked Mary to arrange for Mr. B. to see that particular house. As you may have guessed, Mr. B. saw the house, liked it, and they bought it at once. This was certainly an easy sale for Mary.

Had the first salesperson made only one call to Mrs. B. to review what she liked and didn't like, she would have found out how seriously her prospect was interested in that house. In addition, Mrs. B. would have been impressed with her concern and attention and would, no doubt, have remembered her name.

How one agent lost a $1200 commission

The listing agent received a call in response to one of her "unique" ads. She briefly answered the caller's inquiries, but made no attempt to qualify or to make an appointment to show the house. Later on that day, these people stopped by at the open house of the same firm. They mentioned that they were intrigued by the ad and the information they had received in answer to their call. They asked to be shown that house and, sure enough, one visit was all that was necessary. The house was just what they were looking for and they bought it. Of course, the lister lamented not having followed through. This is just one more example of how giving up too soon puts dollars in another agent's pocket.

Freshening up your sales presentation with "sales reserves"

Because you want to stay with your prospect, yet you don't want to become a nuisance, you will be well received when you add something new each time you call back. For example, you might have a new idea that could be different from anything your competitors have presented, or an interesting brochure, a copy of a listing contract, a copy of an offer to purchase contract, new information regarding the mortgage market, or details on changes in the status of properties in the area. You can certainly be creative enough to think of something new and different that will be of interest to your prospect. When you do this, you won't be dull or boring. Your prospects will welcome you. And, of course, every time you are face-to-face with your prospect gives you more of an opportunity to convince him and come away with a signed contract.

How to determine whom to call and when

When you have qualified a prospective buyer (see Chapter 6) and have executed an effective listing presentation (see Chapter 8), you'll know how motivated these people are. The degree of motivation will serve as a good guide for determining your priorities. Naturally, the more urgent the need, the more attention you will want to give. For instance, buyers from out-of-town and sellers who must get their houses sold quickly because of pressing obligations are the ones who get top priority.

From the degree of urgency and your ability to fulfill their requirements, you can rate your prospects accordingly. After you have determined this, keep some simple records for reference instead of relying on your memory.

Keeping simple records for profitable follow-up

Because real estate agents can get very busy with daily phone calls and interruptions, and because they are involved in many aspects of the business, such as making appointments, showing, listing, and processing their sold properties, some find it handy to keep a daily journal and, at the end of each day, transfer the important matters to their appropriate files. This method gives them a double-check on all information.

If you have specific data forms for listing, qualifying, and processing sales, you can make notes on them, grade them, and then file them accordingly.

Whatever method you use, it will be very helpful to review your records, check your appointment calendar on the evening before or very early in the morning, and decide whom you plan to call and when. For this purpose, any form similar to "Things to Do Today" (page 26) will be convenient.

"If you want to set records, keep records."

Steps to take after the sale

In this area alone, many real estate salespeople make costly mistakes by not following through all the way. Here are steps you can take to prevent problems, save the sale, and at the same time cement a good relationship with buyers and sellers.

After the initial sale—the listing—keep in touch with the seller. Report regularly on action, lack of action, and what you are doing about it. After the buyer and seller have signed the offer to purchase contract, do the following:

1. Immediately congratulate each of them on their wise decisions.

2. Explain briefly what procedures will follow.

3. Keep a copy of the contract in your file. Check and verify that the terms are carried out as specified in the contract.

4. Keep in close contact with the buyers. Make certain that they are doing what they are supposed to do, such as making additional deposit or applying for a mortgage. Notify the seller and the listing office of this information. (If another office is the selling agent, get the information from him.)

5. In the file, keep a complete record regarding matters pertaining to the closing of the sale. (See sample Closing Checklist on page 187.)

6. Check, verify, record, and confirm all matters. Even though some item might be someone else's responsibility, you can't always depend on others. In some situations, oral confirmations may not be adequate or reliable, so you'll find it wiser and safer to ask for written confirmations, just as you would request receipts of payments for record purposes.

7. Keep buyer, seller, selling agent, and attorneys informed about each step in the transaction.

8. Contact each attorney and the lending institution to find out how you can assist them in expediting the paper work.

9. Find out ahead of time and notify those involved about the date, time, and place for closing, date of possession, money disbursements, and money buyer has to come up with at the closing.

If you do these things, your closings will go smoothly, there won't be any blow-ups or delays, and everyone, especially the buyer and seller, will be satisfied and relieved.

The danger of taking it for granted

A salesperon often assumes that what seems to be obvious is being taken care of, so he neglects to double-check. My friend Tom, who is an experienced broker, told me about a serious incident that occurred at a closing simply because he had *assumed.*

Before any closing, Tom said, he's very careful about the dollar amount that will cross hands. At this particular closing, he represented the purchaser, an extremely wealthy businessman who had owned and operated a mortgage company. Tom assumed that this purchaser would know to bring his $10,000 in cash or certified check. When it was time for the buyer to pay the moneys due, however, he produced only dividend checks (one for $3000 took nearly a month to clear). The broker was flabbergasted and the attorney looked on in amazement. They could not believe what they were witnessing. Of course, the closing was delayed until all checks were cleared.

Tom says, "I learned a lesson. Never again will I assume anything. I'll make sure. I'll personally double-check every detail and never again take anything for granted."

The sequel—making the most of each closing

The closing goes smoothly. Everyone is happy and goes around thanking everyone else. When the clients thank you for all you have done for them and tell you how much they appreciate it, accept graciously and then politely tell them that they can show their appreciation by letting you know whenever they hear of anyone who wants to sell or buy a house. Say that you would like an opportunity to help others in the same way.

Listing Salesman: _____
Listing Office: _____
Address: _____
Sold by: _____
Date Listed: _____
Date Sold: _____

CLOSING CHECKLIST*

To Be Closed Not Later Than: _____

   Place of Closing: _____

   Purchaser:

      Name as title is to be taken _____
      Address for Deed _____
      Present Address/Purchaser _____
      Telephone: _____ Attorney: _____
      Atty's Telephone: _____ Atty's Address _____
      Atty's Secretary: _____   _____

Seller:

      Name _____
      Current Address: _____
      Telephone: _____ Attorney: _____
      Attorney's Address: _____
      Atty's Telephone: _____ Sec'y: _____

Address of Property: _____

Abstract:

      Located at _____ Telephone: _____
      Ordered by _____ Date
      Delivered to _____ Date _____

1st Mortgagee:

      Name _____ Telephone: _____
      Address: _____ Spoke with: _____

2nd Mortgagee:

      Name: _____ Address: _____
      Telephone: _____ Spoke with: _____

Insurance Company: _____ Agent: _____

Roof Inspection by: _____ Telephone: _____

      Date Ordered: _____ Rec'd: _____ Representative: _____

Termite Inspection by: _____ Telephone: _____

      Date Ordered: _____ Rec'd: _____ Representative: _____

Roof Inspection Report Sent to _____ Date: _____

Termite Inspection Report Sent to _____ Date: _____

Take Note: _____

New Mtg. Information: _____

_____

When you express your appreciation of your clients' cooperation, commenting on what a pleasure it was to work with them, let
them know that you intend to keep in touch with them. They'll
expect it. It's up to you to follow through and reap the additional
rewards of repeat business and referrals.

How one call resulted in two "hot" listings totaling $96,000

After the first of the year, I call each family whose house I sold
during the previous year to remind them to file for their Homestead Tax Exemption before the first of March. It was during one
such call that the satisfied customer said, "Oh, by the way, you
might call my son Dick. He's trying to get his house sold and
hasn't had much luck. We told him about you, but you know how
children are, they don't always pay attention to what parents say.
Give him a call anyway."

Reluctantly, Dick agreed to an appointment. He had misgiv-
ings about talking to any agent whose office was not in his
immediate area. Nonetheless, the interview did result in a listing.

The following Sunday, the house was held open and sold on
the same day. This surprised Dick, who had had his house listed
for three months with a neighbor's real estate agent. He suggested
that I call on his friend, who lived in another area and was in a
similar predicament. His listing, too, had just expired.

Dick's friend's house was an eight-year-old, four bedroom, two
bath rancher, on a corner with the added attraction of 25 different
exotic plantings. The house was now empty. I convinced the owner
to drop the price by $3000, which placed it within a more realistic
price range. This house sold in two weeks. The total of the two
houses was $96,000.

These two "hot" listings were the result of a routine follow-up
call. You never know how much business can be radiated from
periodic calls to those with whom you have done business. So, if
you follow the rule, "Never forget a customer and never let a
customer forget you," you'll find that it really pays off.

Be sure to follow through by letting the person who gave you
the referral know the results, whether you were successful or not.
This further cements a good relationship and ensures future
referrals.

Always remember the rewards

It is easy to say, "I'll do it another time, maybe tomorrow or next week." When you do this, you are forgetting the rewards. By following through, as advised in this chapter, you'll be richly rewarded with a more successful career.

Checklist for Following Through All the Way

Do you

Give up too soon on selling the seller?

Give up too soon on working with the promising prospective buyer?

Use some "sales reserves" to clinch the sale?

Classify your customers and clients according to their urgent needs and your ability to perform?

As the listing agent, follow a consistent method of reporting back to the seller?

Refrain from assuming anything about either the people or the property?

Have a simple system for recording each day's activity?

Spend some time regularly reviewing your records, to decide whom to call and when?

Systematically contact former accounts for referrals?

Always let the other person know the outcome of the referral?

Remind yourself of the rewards of following through all the way?

Take some definite steps after the sale to avoid costly and frustrating mistakes in processing the sale?

16

Failure to

Attempt Closing Often Enough

If you can't close, you can't sell. It's as simple as that. You can therefore conclude that your success is determined by the number of sales you close. Many salespeople find closing to be one of the toughest problems to face in the real estate business. They are intimidated or frightened by the word *close*. They don't realize that closing is really a simple, obvious, and natural step to selling. All you have to do to become a good closer is to follow the secret system used by the top producers. These champions develop closing consciousness. From the beginning, they are constantly and continuously closing, closing, closing. This makes them winners.

One day at lunch, while discussing the art of closing, Albert, who is a strong closer, told me about a recent sale. He described how he and another salesperson handled the same situation when the buying signals flashed.

Mr. W. came to look at Albert's open house. It was Sunday and his wife was out of town. He loved this house at once, claiming that it had everything he and his wife wanted. There was just one problem: the carpeting throughout the house was blue. That was the one color that did not go with their furnishings. Albert, being alert, asked him if he had any other objections, and found that there were none. At this point, Albert assured Mr. W. that the carpeting need not be a serious problem. New carpeting could be purchased, perhaps even at discount prices, and then they would have the house they wanted with the exact color of their choice. Albert asked if Mr. and Mrs. W. were going to let the little matter of changing the carpeting stand in their way, and forfeit this house that he knew was ideal for them.

Mr. W. was puzzled. He could not understand how his wife had overlooked this house, because she had been looking for some time. A call to her revealed that she had indeed seen that very house with another salesperson. She also felt that it was perfect for them, but, like her husband, had said that she couldn't use blue rugs. Her agent had not suggested changing the carpeting and had gone on to show her other houses. Mrs. W. agreed that it made good sense to go ahead, buy the house, and choose new carpeting of another color.

As you can see, Albert succeeded because, when he spotted strong buying signals, he decided to try to close one more time, and did so by offering a plausible solution to the problem.

THE BENEFITS YOU'LL GAIN

1. You'll acquire confidence, the first essential ingredient in successful selling. This confidence will transmit itself to your prospects.
2. You'll speed up your closings, closing twice as soon and twice as often.
3. You won't subscribe to the mistaken belief that you must wait for the psychological moment or else you'll lose the sale.
4. You'll find closing to be a simple, obvious, and natural step in the sale.
5. You'll seek more challenges, aim higher, and set greater goals no matter how much you sell.
6. You'll not only obtain more listings, but you'll also find that you'll be selling them.
7. You'll overcome the prospect's tendency to procrastinate and his fear of performing now.
8. You won't be just an order taker—you'll sell on purpose, not by accident.
9. You'll be a pro—you'll think "closing"—you'll think "success."
10. You'll sell and you'll get paid.

TECHNIQUES YOU CAN USE TO GAIN THESE BENEFITS

Think closing, think success

Many salespeople do a good selling job up until the close, but then they fail to help their prospects make a decision. Very often, it is the fear of rejection that prompts some salespeople to wait, hoping that the prospect will finally say, "Yes, we'll go ahead."

The first step you can take to overcome this fear is to close in your own mind first. Then it is much easier to help your prospect make up his mind. It becomes a matter of attitude rather than aptitude. Here are a few simple suggestions to assist you in adjusting your thinking:

- Remember that people love to buy.
- Recognize that selling does not consist of talking someone into doing something he doesn't want to do. Selling just involves making it easy for your prospect to do something he enjoys doing.
- Realize that you are primarily a problem solver, rather than a salesperson.
- Remind yourself to think "closing." You might use a 3 x 5 card, with writing in bold letters that says, *"Think closing! Today I am going to close!"* Glance at the card frequently, as you gather your notes, plan your day, and prepare your presentation to list, to show, or to negotiate.

As the saying goes, "Success comes in cans, failure comes in can'ts." Therefore, once you condition yourself to *think* you can close, you'll discover that you *can* close.

How one salesperson's fear of closing changed the newlyweds' plan to buy

When an agent sees that a buyer is interested and doesn't help the buyer come to a conclusion, he often uses the excuse, "I didn't want to pressure them." This was Mildred's problem.

Mildred, who was a broker, went out on several weekends with a young couple who were looking for their first home. Each weekend they found one house that they liked very much, but ended up saying the usual, "We want to think about it some more." Mildred knew that they liked all of the houses and felt that any one of them would be satisfactory, but because it was their first home she felt that they must be absolutely certain. She didn't encourage them to decide then and there. Weeks went by and they still had not made up their minds. Finally, one weekend they announced, "We've decided not to buy, so we aren't going to look any more." At that point they were completely confused, they had seen so many houses that they couldn't possibly decide. Had Mildred helped or hurt them?

When to close—follow the A B C rule

As any successful salesperson knows, there is no one psychological moment to close. While one moment may be better than others, any time may be the right time to close. Closing is the art of getting your prospects to agree with you on a series of positive points. The series consists of little sales you make as you go along. These sales form a link in the chain, beginning with making the appointment, which leads to either selling the seller to list or convincing the buyer to buy, followed by presenting and negotiating an offer, which finally joins the links together and closes the sale for keeps.

To accomplish this, here's a simple guide you can follow:

- *Start your presentation with a closing remark:* "If you see what you like, is there any reason why you can't buy it today?"
- *Continue closing:* "Would you prefer a 30-day closing or would 60 days be better for you?"
- *Finalize your presentation with a closing action:* "Mr. and Mrs. Buyer, based on what you have told me, may I suggest that we go ahead and include those items that are important to you?"

A secretary I know says that she always knew her boss was a quick-thinking, go-getting salesman. But she never knew how quick-thinking and go-getting he was until the other day when the telephone rang in their real estate office and a soft female voice asked, "Do you sell maternity clothes?" Realizing that she had the wrong number, the boss was quick to reply, "No, ma'am, but could we interest you in a larger house?"

Where is the best place to close?

Whenever you have a prospect who is ready, willing, and able to perform, that is the time to act quickly before buyer's jitters set in. Everyone is fearful at the moment of making a decision, but this is especially true when the decision is a big one. Since it is a matter of timing, you'll find that "when" is more important than "where." Therefore, you should close wherever you can do so promptly and conveniently without interruptions or interference from others. This could be:

- In the home.
- In the car.
- At a nearby location, such as a restaurant or shopping center.
- In your office.

Circumstances will dictate the place where you can close most expeditiously.

I had heard of contracts being written on the hoods of automobiles, but I wasn't sure it was done. However, one evening I found myself in that very situation.

A young couple met me at a shopping center to see some houses in a nearby neighborhood. They found a house that caught their fancy, but their two-year-old twins were tired, hungry, and crying. They had a 15-mile trip back to their apartment and my office was almost as far away in another direction. It occurred to me that if they left then, one of two things might happen. Either the house could be sold, or, by the time they got home and thought it over, they might have some doubts and decide to look some more. So I politely pleaded for just a few more minutes, enough time to scribble in the details on a contract to purchase the house. Right on the hood of my car I did just that and made the sale. You too might one day find yourself doing the same thing in order to save a sale.

Four basic steps to creating an atmosphere of acceptance

Here's a simple method you can use to win your prospect's approval and get the order:

1. Use the prospect's name frequently. People love to hear the sound of their own names.
2. Ask a closing question, the answer to which confirms that your prospect is ready to go ahead and purchase the property or list it.
3. Listen very closely to the answer. (Many salespeople fail here.)
4. Write the order or go back to selling and repeat these steps.

When you put these four basic steps into practice you will multiply the sales possibilities.

Using closing questions to put your prospect in a favorable frame of mind

The star sales agent, always conscious of closing, uses a time-tested method to get his prospect to agree. He closes on minor matters first. You can do this by asking questions that you know your prospect will answer positively. You merely feed back to him the items which he has indicated that he wants and needs, so you know he'll agree. For instance:

- "Having easy access to public transportation is important to you isn't it?"
- "You and your family will certainly enjoy having your own pool, won't you?"
- "You would like the washer, dryer, and refrigerator included, wouldn't you?"
- "You said that you wanted to close not later than July 15, isn't that right?"
- "You are planning on applying for an 80 percent mortgage, aren't you?"

In essence, you are verifying and committing your prospect to those details to which he has previously agreed. As you can see, each statement has a question attached to it which encourages a favorable response. When a person keeps saying "yes" without realizing it, he is being lulled into a favorable frame of mind. Studies show and successful salespeople confirm the fact that when you get "yes" answers on a series of minor points first, you'll have a better chance of closing on major points later on.

Persuading prospects with powerful sales techniques

Offering a choice forces a decision. There are times when you don't want either a "yes" or "no" answer, yet you do want your customer to commit himself. In such situations, it works well to ask questions that will give him a chance to choose between two alternatives.

- "Mrs. Seller, will it be more convenient to see your home tomorrow morning or afternoon?"
- "Are you planning on refinancing, or assuming the existing mortgage?"
- "Would you prefer to make your initial deposit $1000 or $2000?"

When you ask such questions, the prospect is forced to make a decision. Which answer they choose doesn't matter; the important thing is that they have decided on something. So, whatever the choice, you will still be closing.

When the sale founders, save it by changing the subject. This technique is extremely effective when your prospect is interested yet seems to be hesitating, wondering and worrying about whether he is making the right decision. You can change the subject easily by saying, "By the way," and then following with something you know will interest him.

If you're in the office, this is a good time to offer the prospects a cup of coffee, but if you're out in the field they'll welcome a stop for a snack, lunch, or dinner. It's a great way to temporarily change the subject. And when you do get back to selling, your prospects will be relaxed and receptive to making a favorable decision.

Convince with a third-party story. This is another powerful technique you can use effectively to convince an undecided buyer or seller. Tell a true story about a similar situation or produce a testimonial letter from a satisfied customer or client, and you'll see how effective it will be in making the sale or getting the listing. Of course, the story must be relevant and deal with something with which the listener can instinctively identify. In other words, in order for you to use this technique properly, you must tell the right story, in the right way, to the right person, at the right time. (See Chapter 13 for a complete discussion of storytelling.)

Summarize reasons to buy now. The summary technique is one of the most effective methods you can use to help a prospect make that final decision to buy. When you see that your prospects are interested, yet can't quite make up their minds, try using the summary technique:

"Mr. and Mrs. Prospect, let's review together what you like and don't like about this house."

Then proceed by writing in one column the reasons "Why Buy." List the features and benefits that appealed to them. Everything must be from their point of view. This makes it both believable and acceptable. Then, in the next column list the few reasons "Why Not Buy."

You'll notice that once you put these reasons down on paper for them to see, people usually realize that the list of reasons to buy far outweigh the few reasons not to. When you summarize all of the pros and cons in this fashion, you are helping them to crystallize their thoughts so that they can comfortably reach the logical conclusion to go ahead now.

In Chapter 5, in the discussion on using feedback advantageously, you will find a detailed example of the use of this summary technique to close a sale.

How to lock in the sale

The word *why* may be just the word you need to nudge your prospects into making a decision. Perhaps you have used the summary technique, but your prospects are still hesitating, or maybe you have filled in all the information on the contract only to hear, "We didn't say we were going ahead." When this happens, try asking, "Why? Why do you hesitate? ... Why not go ahead now?"

If this does not bring about the desired results, follow it up with one of the most effective closing techniques ever devised. After you have heard them out, hesitate for a moment, and then ask, "In addition to that, Mr. and Mrs. Prospect, isn't there something else, some other reason that makes you hesitate to go ahead and buy this house right now?"

You will discover that whatever they answer to the first "why" is something that sounds reasonable, but is just an excuse. However, the second reason is the real reason, one you might never suspect. Once you uncover the true objection, you are in a good position to handle it and close.

Let's is another power-packed phrase. The combination of these two words, "let us," really means "you and I together." It invites immediate cooperation and is a great way to lead your prospects' thinking.

- *"Let's* see what we can do to hold this contract together."
- *"Let's* put it down on paper."
- *"Let's* go back and take one more look."

What if is another phrase that locks in any prospect:

- *"What if* I can get the buyer to come up with $2000 more. Would you then be willing to go ahead?"
- *"What if* I bring you a buyer who is willing to pay your price plus commission. Would that be acceptable to you?"
- *"What if* we find just what you are looking for. Will you buy it today?"

"What if" is one more potent tool you can use to make it easy to obtain definite commitments.

More ways to close sales

The words *how, what, when, who,* and *where* can be used skillfully to imply acceptance:

- *"How* would you like your name recorded on the deed?"
- *"What* do you want included in your offer to purchase?"
- *"When* would you like to move in?"
- *"Who* else will have to be consulted to make a decision?"
- *"Where* would you plan to put your lovely piano?"

When you make these words part of your selling vocabulary and use them frequently throughout your presentation, you will soon discover their magical power in closing.

The question, silence, and then the signature

After you ask a closing question, you should stay silent and wait until they answer. For some salespeople, this suspense is too much to endure. They feel compelled to come forth and say something. They completely ruin the effect of the vitally important question they just asked. As a result, the question is wasted. You need to remain absolutely silent, no matter how long it takes. It is difficult to do and it does require plenty of practice before it becomes a habit, but it will pay off, and is particularly powerful in producing a positive response.

The next logical step is, without another word, to obtain the signature on the bottom line: "Please write your name exactly as it appears on the top of the page."

Having the contract in full view makes it easier to close

Concern about filling out any contract is mostly in the mind of the salesperson. Today, people are accustomed to seeing order forms. They also know that, until they sign, they are not under any obligation. However, great closers realize that a written commitment is a natural step in any sale. So they always have their order forms—contracts—handy and ready to use.

These star salespeople use the assumptive technique to confirm the details in writing. It might go like this:

"What is your full name, Mr. Buyer? And yours, Mrs. Buyer?"

"Let's put down on paper those items you want."

"You would like the drapes and carpeting included, isn't that so?"

"You said you wanted to be sure to close no later than July 15, correct? Let's be sure to include that."

As you go along, ask them what other details they would like included. Give them a chance to volunteer this information even if you know it. People love to feel that they are buying, not being sold.

Getting your prospect to participate is an easy way to write up a buy or sell agreement. More than once I have asked a seller to fill in the information on a listing agreement because my handwriting is so poor. The husband is the one who usually volunteers to do it. One seller even insisted on using his typewriter. Whenever you get a prospect to participate, he feels and acts as a partner working with you.

Objections—opportunities to close

To some real estate salespeople, objections are obstacles they think they have to overcome before they can close. However, when you realize that objections can actually be helpful and not harmful to closing the sale, you will react differently. For instance, objections can:

- Indicate interest.
- Denote a desire to be reassured.
- Provide the very reason to buy now.
- Bring clues out of the closet and furnish important clues to the prospect's thinking.
- Reveal the progress you are making.

"I want to think it over" is a plea for reassurance. It really means, "I'm not quite sure that I will be doing the right thing. Please tell me more."

"I don't make snap judgments," or, "I want to sleep on it," means, "Why is it to my advantage to buy—or sell—now?"

"The price is too high," means, "Will I get good value?" or, "Can I afford the payments?"

"Perhaps we should wait until prices—interest rates—come down," means, "Will I be better off to take a chance and wait, or will I gain more by going ahead?"

When you treat objections as an aid and not as a barrier to a sale, it will strengthen your presentation and increase your chances of closing.

What to say when they say, "I'd like to have my relatives look at it"

When your customer says, "I'd like to have my relatives look at it," you might reply, "May I ask if you need their approval before going ahead? Are these relatives going to contribute toward the financing?" The answer is almost always, "No, we'll be handling it on our own, but we'd just like for them to see it."

You can continue by saying, "Mr. and Mrs. Buyer, from experience we have learned that it makes a big difference what you say when you call in friends or relatives to look at a house you like. If you tell them you'd like them to see a house you both like and have decided to buy, they will view it quite differently than if you say you'd like them to look at a particular house that you are considering and you would like their opinion of it. In the latter case, your relatives will feel compelled to be critical and they will deliberately find something wrong in order to justify their criticism. Unfortunately, their complaints are generally from their own points of view and not from yours."

Then add, "You remind me of another young couple who were in the same predicament. These people passed up the house they really wanted. After much frustration and some time later, they finally ended up settling for something they liked much less. I wouldn't like the same thing to happen to you.

"Tell me, Mr. and Mrs. Buyer, how *will* you feel if someone else buys this house in the meantime?" This question applies a popular technique of warning the prospect that he might lose something which he could just as easily gain. Whenever you use this technique properly, the prospect usually decides to buy rather than taking the chance of losing out.

How to handle the stall: "I'd like to consult my attorney first"

If the buyers want to consult their attorney, they should be encouraged to do so. Remember *caveat emptor*—"buyer beware." However, you can avoid unnecessary contract changes, prevent problems, and in some instances save the sale by first offering to contact their attorney for them. If they agree, you have a golden opportunity to build good rapport with the attorney. When you inform the attorney that his clients have decided on a purchase of some property and would like him to review their contract to make certain that it is legally correct, he will be receptive and cooperative, and you will be off to a good start.

If, however, your prospects prefer to contact the attorney themselves, impress upon them:

1) The importance of contacting the attorney immediately in order to avoid the possible serious consequences that could be caused by any delay.

2) The prime purpose of consulting their attorney at this time is to have him check the legal wording of the contract. Explain that they are neither asking nor paying the attorney for any real estate advice, such as an opinion on the price of the property or the terms of the contract.

When you carefully explain these two points to your prospects, you reduce the number of problems, pave the way for a smoother transaction, and ultimately save the sale.

Ask and ye shall receive

You may have heard the story about a salesman who had memorized his presentation. Later, when he found himself face-to-face with a prospect, he went through his presentation book, but nothing happened, so he repeated the presentation, and again nothing happened. Finally, after the third time, he stopped and asked, "Why won't you buy?" The customer heaved a sigh of relief and answered, "I thought you'd never ask!"

As you can see, customers expect you to ask for the order.

If you want a favor, you *ask*. If you want your prayers answered, you *ask*. To get anywhere, you frequently *ask* in order to arrive there. All the technique and ability you develop in the sophisticated art of selling is virtually useless unless it is accompanied by the capability of *asking* at the right time for the listing and *asking* for the offer.

As babies, we *asked* (by crying) for almost everything—a bottle, a diaper change, a security blanket. As we mature we still *ask*, but in a more refined or subtle way. Sometimes—for some strange reason—we get hung up and think that *asking* is bad. We might even make some dumb remark like, "I'm too proud to *ask*."

Asking is just as important to adult survival as it is for a baby. Try it! *Ask* for the listing. *Ask* for the offer. Why not begin today?

Which closing technique to use when

Although this chapter has covered a variety of closing techniques, you will find more material on closing specific situations in the previous chapters. These too can contribute considerably toward developing your closing consciousness, since they cover situations from making appointments to making your sale stay sold.

You may still wonder which technique would be best for you to use and when. After you familiarize yourself with the various techniques, choose the ones that you feel comfortable using and the ones that work for you. Your temperament and the temperament of your prospect will, of course, influence you in determining which technique to use and when. Consequently, when you adjust the closing techniques to your personality, to your presentation, and to your prospects, you will, most assuredly, multiply your sales possibilities.

Checklist for Increasing Your Rate of Closing

Do you consistently try to develop closing consciousness by
    Conditioning yourself to think "closing"—think "success"?
    Have the attitude that you will close?

Do you attempt to close each selling situation by
    Starting your sales talk with a closing remark?
    Continuing to close during the entire interview?
    Taking some final closing action?

Do you put the prospect in a receptive frame of mind by closing on minor points first?

Do you close wherever you are, whenever the prospect is ready?

Do you include in the sales talk the four basic steps for closing:
    Use the prospect's name frequently?
    Ask closing question?
    Listen closely to answer?
    Write the order or repeat steps 1, 2, and 3?

Do you use various tested closing techniques?

    Use alternate choice questions to force a commitment?

    Change the subject to relax the prospect at a tense moment?

    Convince the prospect by summarizing reasons to buy now?

Do you try to get your prospect to reveal the real reason for hesitating by using "Why," and then, "Isn't there something else?"

Do you include in your closing remarks the cooperating words, "let's" and "what if"?

Do you refrain from saying anything until after your prospect has completely answered your closing question?

Do you treat objections as opportunities to close, not as obstacles?

Do you have a reasonable response ready when the prospect says, "I'd like to have my relatives look at it" or, "I'd like to consult my attorney first"?

Do you keep the contract in full view, ready to use?

Do you ask for the order several times, and then one more time?

17

Failure to

Take Maximum Advantage

of the Telephone

The telephone is a marvelous method of communication. Next to being face-to-face with a person, the telephone is still the best medium available to a real estate salesperson for the purpose of giving and receiving information. But, like computers and other great modern inventions, the telephone is only as effective and efficient as the person who operates it. When you use it properly, the telephone can be an extremely valuable tool. Otherwise, a phone call can be an exercise in futility.

You should, however, accept the challenge, overcome the fears, and make the most of this handy tool.

THE BENEFITS YOU'LL GAIN

1. You'll make friends and create goodwill.
2. You'll get a warm reception from the other person. He'll respond favorably.
3. Your callers will cooperate more readily.
4. You'll make more valid appointments with prospects to list and show properties.

5. You'll discover that the telephone is a time saver, an energy saver, a money saver, and a sales saver.

6. You'll free up time for other important and productive matters.

7. And, most importantly, you can attain peak production. You'll be a real pro.

Because the person at the other end of the phone cannot see you, it is your voice that represents you and creates an impression. Therefore, it is not only what you say that influences the listener, but how you say it. Your manner in handling the call either invites interest or turns the other person off.

TECHNIQUES YOU CAN USE TO GAIN THESE BENEFITS

Disciplined use of the telephone for best results

It is very easy to fall into the trap of using the phone merely as a time filler when there doesn't seem to be anything pressing at the moment. But a convenient time for making phone calls rarely ever comes. There are always excuses you can find for not doing it now. On the other hand, if you discipline yourself and plan a rigid schedule of a prescribed number of calls to make each day, you will soon see the beneficial results.

A routine that generally works well is to set aside specific days and times of the day for making calls on listing appointments, prospecting, and call-backs, according to the importance of the calls. Business calls to attorneys, lending institutions, and brokers can be made conveniently between 9:00 and 10:00 a.m., at a time that may be too early to call some prospects or sellers. If you are contacting working homeowners for either appointments or call-backs, you can generally reach them between 5:00 and 7:00 in the evening.

To make the most of your telephone time, it is helpful the night before to assemble the pertinent details involving each call. This would include the names and phone numbers of the people you plan to call, in addition to notes on what you plan to say.

Whatever time schedule you do arrange, your aim, of course, is to make the calls as productive as possible. This involves preparing and conditioning yourself before each calling session. Regardless of the number of disappointments, promise yourself that you'll continue and complete your list. After a while, when you have followed such a routine faithfully, you'll be pleased and amazed at the results.

A friendly smile in your voice will get you a warm response

If you stop and think about your own personal calls, wouldn't you agree that when you get a cheerful greeting of, "Good morning, may I help you?" it starts your conversation and your day off right. On the other hand, how do you feel when someone answers in a gruff, terse tone and says, "We're all out of them," or, "There's nothing we can do about it," and abruptly hangs up? You feel annoyed and angry because that person didn't care to take the trouble to discuss your situation or perhaps suggest an alternative solution.

That's exactly what happens when you are the one who is making or receiving the call. Therefore, when you approach each call with happy thoughts such as, "Here's an opportunity to help solve someone's problem," or, "Perhaps I'll make an interesting friend," the person you are talking to will open up and freely tell you what you want to know.

Some salespeople get thrown by the very thought of using the phone. They find it difficult to sound natural. They are uncomfortable and they sound stilted. If this is your problem, try to imagine that you are about to talk to a friend with whom you are eager to share some exciting information. You might approach each call as though you were welcoming a friend with a warm, firm handshake. When you do this, you'll not only sound cheerful, but you will be talking enthusiastically. Such a manner is generally infectious, and the listener will also become friendly and interested.

If you aren't sure how you sound, or if you aren't getting the right response, try taping a few calls. What is your reaction? Do you have that friendly smile in your voice? As another check, you might ask an associate or your broker to listen in on some of your calls and then let you know how you come across.

Controlling conversation to maintain direction of the call

Whether you are calling for an appointment or discussing other matters, it is easy for your conversation to drift off. Yet, because time is so important to any salesperson, you really can't afford to do this. You can overcome this tendency to talk on and on—a common weakness among real estate salespeople—by being brief and to the point.

One simple solution is to prepare some guidelines to follow and adhere to them closely. These guidelines could consist of notes, questions, and information that you may need for each call you make. After you cover each item as briefly as possible, glance down at the next question or point you want to make and cover it immediately. Continue to concentrate on covering those items you have planned. With any presentation that is planned, you'll stay on the track. In other words, you'll be the one in the driver's seat.

Using the phone to get appointments, not to sell

No one will doubt that the telephone is one of the easiest and most effective tools any real estate salesperson can use to make appointments. But if you forget that it's just the appointment you are after, you can ruin it.

Even though you may have developed the ability to be enthusiastic and friendly, remember to refrain from being carried away when they ask specific questions about the service you are offering, the properties they may be interested in, or the contract that is pending. Otherwise, whatever additional information you volunteer can be just enough to kill your sale.

When the prospect asks about some detail, you can respond by saying, "This is one of the things I want to go over with you. It's too difficult to discuss these matters on the phone. When will it be most convenient to meet with you, at 6:00 tonight, or would 7:30 be better?"

Before you start making calls for appointments, you will find it advantageous to remind yourself to be brief and tactful as you concentrate on getting the appointment and nothing more. In other words, save the selling for later when it can do you some good.

Fred W. Jenkins has demonstrated all types of inquiries in his program, "Real Estate in Action." The following example is used in his program for Realtors.

Inquiry About an Advertisement*

Phone rings once: "Fred Jenkins, Realtor; Fred Jenkins speaking."

---

*From the book, *How to Increase Sales and Put Yourself Across by Telephone*, by Mona Ling. ©1963, by Mona Ling. Published by Prentice-Hall, Inc., Englewood Cliffs, New Jersey 07632.

Mr. Carter: "This is Cliff Carter. I wonder if you'd be good enough to give me a little information about the house you advertised in last night's paper for $48,500?"

Fred: "Why, certainly, Mr. Carter, I'll be glad to. It's a well-designed colonial, in excellent condition, situated in the Bradley district. Where do you live, Mr. Carter?"

Mr. Carter: "We live on Moon Drive. We've been here about a year and are not too familiar with the city."

Fred: "In that case, would you like to have a copy of our city map? It shows all the sections of town, the schools, public buildings, golf courses, transportation facilities, as well as many other important locations. I'll be glad to send you a copy. C-A-R-T-E-R. Is that correct?"

Mr. Carter: "Yes. The street number is 2906 Moon Drive."

Fred: "Thank you, Mr. Carter. If you will tell me your particular needs, I will do my best to help you. It will help me to know the type of house you now live in, and what you like and don't like about it."

Mr. Carter: "Well, we now have a four-room apartment, on which we've given notice to move in 60 days, and we want to get into a six- or seven-room colonial."

Fred: "We have a fine selection of houses this size. Would you mind telling me if you plan to pay cash for a house, or would you want a mortgage?"

Mr. Carter: "Thanks for the compliment, but $10,000 cash is what we hoped to buy a house with."

Fred: "That's fine, Mr. Carter. We should have no trouble in arranging everything so as to make your change of address a real pleasure. You will want to start the ball rolling as soon as possible, won't you?"

Mr. Carter: "Yes, we'd like to get started right away on making the change."

Fred: "In that case, you and Mrs. Carter should arrange to come to the office so we can determine what your needs are and discuss some of our choice houses. Which would be better, this afternoon or this evening?"

Mr. Carter: "I guess this evening would be better. How about eight o'clock?"

Fred: "Eight o'clock would be fine with me. Thank you very much for your information. I'll see you here in my office at eight. Good-bye, Mr. Carter."

Mr. Carter: "Good-bye." (Hangs up first.)

Notice the objectives that Fred Jenkins achieved in this inquiry. By ending each statement with a question, Fred now knows:

- Where the Carters live.
- How familiar they are with the city.
- The number of rooms and what type of house they are interested in.
- Their reason for moving.
- How motivated they are.
- The amount of money they plan to invest initially.
- A definite appointment has been made to further qualify and counsel the Carters.

What to say when they ask for the address

One of the first questions in response to an ad is usually, "What is the address of the home you have advertised?" Many Realtors train their salespeople to evade giving out this information. Some agents are told to say, "The seller requested us not to give the address out over the phone," or, "It's a company policy not to give out addresses on the telephone." Such responses tend to annoy most people. It's up to you to decide for yourself if you want to be secretive and evasive, hoping to hold on to a possible prospect, or if you want to handle the same question in a way that won't be so irritating, yet can get good results.

When someone asks for the address of a property, an effective way to handle it is to answer in general terms first: "It's in the Kendall Lakes area. Are you familiar with that section? Would you like that location?"

The caller might respond, "Yes, I am familiar with that area, but we don't want to go so far out."

That takes care of the address without evading the question and now you can continue qualifying the caller in a friendly fashion. As you know, this sort of thing happens frequently on ad calls. The house referred to by the caller does not generally meet his specific needs. So there is no reason to be secretive or to waste time by continuing to describe a house which does not fit.

If, however, the answer is, "Yes, that is where we'd like to be," then you can follow with the next qualifying question: "The owners are asking $65,000, is that the price range you are considering?"

You may finish qualifying the caller without making an appointment, because the caller may prefer to ride by, look at the outside, and examine the neighborhood. You should then politely give the address, encourage the caller to drive by with his or her family, and, if they do, you'll have a better chance of making a sale:

"That's a good idea, Mrs. Buyer. Please call me back and let me know what you think of this house, whether or not it appeals to you and your husband. And if you like, I'll arrange to show it to you. May I also suggest that, while you're driving around the neighborhood, if you see any interesting houses that have Realtors' "For Sale" signs, jot down the information and I'll check them out for you. Now that I know your specific requirements, I can do the research and arrange to show you only those houses which sound like what you are looking for. I'll be glad to set up appointments for a time that will be most convenient for you and Mr. Buyer.

"As you probably know, the purchasing prices the owners ask are exactly the same for everyone. That's the reason why they and all of the brokers always cooperate willingly. It won't cost you any more, but my doing the checking for you can save you a considerable amount of time and trouble. You would like that, Mrs. Buyer, wouldn't you?"

You have probably won Mrs. Buyer's confidence and cooperation. You haven't wasted her time or yours. And if she and her husband pick out houses that they'd like to see, you've gained a good prospect. As you know, a person who calls in response to a sign is half sold, so you're halfway to making the sale.

How to handle calls to attorneys

Because your time is also valuable, you cannot afford to wait for hours or days to talk to an attorney. Yet, lawyers themselves will tell you that they are great procrastinators and this includes returning calls. When you need to get information from a lawyer, the key to the situation is his secretary. She knows not only his whereabouts, but also what he has to do and when. She is the one who plans his schedule and does most of the paper work. In fact, an attorney relies on his secretary to do much more than answer the phone and take dictation. Therefore, with that in mind, you should try to cultivate her friendship. She can and will save you a lot of time and grief.

Initially, identify yourself, giving your name and the company you represent, and briefly state your business. Be professional by speaking slowly and distinctly, friendly but firmly: "Joan, I need some information from Mr. Attorney. Perhaps you can help me. Do you know if he has received the abstract on the A.'s house, or what has happened to it?"

Joan will probably know the answer, but if not, she'll most likely offer to find out and call you back. Before hanging up, ask, "Joan, can you give me some idea how long that will take? We must get it to XYZ Savings and Loan as soon as possible. They claim it is holding up the closing. Thanks very much."

In the case of specific information that only the attorney can answer, you might say, "Joan, we have a problem on the sale of the A.'s house. I must talk to Mr. Attorney as soon as possible. How can we get in touch with him?"

Joan will probably volunteer some solution. She may even tell you how she'll reach him, where, and when. If, however, Mr. Attorney does not contact you as she said he would, call back again, politely but frantically saying, "Joan, I hate to bother you, but Mr. Attorney has not called yet. What can we do?" Joan will do everything possible to help.

Satisfactorily settling problems between the buyer and the seller

Sometimes, after a contract has been signed and accepted, problems arise between the buyer and the seller. If this does happen, it is generally wiser to let their attorneys handle the differences. You should either call the attorney or recommend to the party you represent that they call him and explain the problem. This usually brings about speedy and satisfactory results for two reasons:

1. Lawyers readily cooperate with each other. They like to talk to each other to iron out any differences.

2. Clients listen to whatever their lawyers advise them. They feel that that is what they are paying them for.

When you leave it up to the lawyers, there are also extra bonuses in it for you:

• You win points with the lawyer. You feed his ego, and he feels that it is a mark of respect for his position as advisor to his client.

- You save the time and are spared the nuisance of being involved in the dispute.
- You can comfortably continue your good relationship with both parties—buyer and seller—who end up satisfied, rather than hostile.
- You can count on the closing being smoother and taking place sooner.

One example that comes to mind was a situation in which the contract stated that the seller was responsible for seeing that the house was in non-leaking condition. There were discrepancies in the roof estimates. One roofer estimated a cost as high as $3000. The seller balked, and the buyer insisted, until finally the real estate agent representing the seller suggested that the seller should turn the matter over to his attorney and let the two attorneys settle it. It worked and the dispute was resolved. The seller agreed to pay $1000 toward any repairs that the buyer wanted to make, and the sale closed as scheduled.

Helpful hints to improve your telephone personality

Since the person with whom you are speaking on the telephone can't see your appearance or your facial expressions, your voice will be your only opportunity to convey your personality. You can understand why it is so vital to develop a pleasing personality, one that makes you sound alert and attractive, warm and friendly, and genuinely interested in being of service.

Here are some suggestions for doing just that:

- When the phone rings, answer on the first ring. People don't like to be kept waiting, and answering promptly gives the impression that you are efficient.
- Identify yourself in a pleasant, positive, proud manner. A voice that sounds happy and helpful encourages confidence.
- Speak slowly and distinctly, but without hesitation. If the caller has to strain to follow what you are saying, you may lose your customer.
- Address the person by name frequently. People enjoy the sound of their own names.
- Maintain a conversational tone without making irrelevant comments.

- Use simple, everyday language. When the caller doesn't understand, he may turn you off.
- Show that you are a good listener. Don't make the caller repeat himself. Allow him time to express himself.
- Demonstrate that you care with a courteous, considerate attitude—little things that count: Use plenty of *please, thank you,* and *may I suggest?* If you have someone on hold, don't delay. When making calls at odd hours, ask if it is a convenient time. Let the other person hang up first.

Calls are precious—make them pay off

To reap the full benefit of the call, immediately after you hang up, mark down the time and place of the appointment on your calendar and take complete notes of the conversation so that you can keep them on file for future reference. If you wait to do this until later, or trust to memory, you may forget some important fact and some valuable and vital information may escape you. This could make the difference in the outcome of the call.

After calls to or from attorneys' offices, mortgage companies, or lending institutions, it is wise to ask for the name of the person to whom you are talking and his or her position. Make a record of this, together with the date and details covered in the conversation. This information may be valuable at some future date, either for reference or proof in case of any controversy. It's like having a signed receipt on hand to use if and when you need it. Of course, if you need to call again, it is more efficient to be able to ask for the person who is already familiar with the situation. This not only saves time, but it also prevents confusion and duplication of effort.

In order to make sure that you are taking the maximum advantage of the telephone, you can check yourself periodically. Review your notes and records, evaluate your performance, and you'll notice your weaknesses and your strengths. You'll certainly want to continue with the methods that work well for you. On the other hand, you'll want to discard or change those that do not in order to improve and make the most of your telephone calls.

Checklist for Making Maximum Use of the Telephone

Do you plan what you are going to say on the telephone?

Do you devote certain days and certain times of the day to making calls?

Listing appointments?

Showing property?

Call-backs?

Use morning hours, 9:00 to 10:00 a.m., to call attorneys, lending institutions, or other brokers?

Do you put a smile in your voice while talking on the telephone?

Do you talk easily and eagerly on the phone, as you would to a friend?

Do you get a warm response?

Do you stay on track by using prepared questions, notes, or checklists?

Do you refrain from using the telephone to sell?

Do you know how you'll respond when the caller asks for an address?

Do you find it easy to handle telephone calls to attorneys?

Utilize their secretaries to get information, get a time for call-backs, resolve problems?

Do you answer incoming calls by identifying yourself in a pleasant, helpful manner?

Speak slowly and distinctly so that people understand you?

Use the caller's name frequently?

Maintain a conversational tone without drifting from the subject?

Use simple language?

Stay alert—avoid making the caller repeat himself?

Let the other person speak freely?

Take time to be courteous by using common courtesy words, not keeping the caller on hold for too long, avoiding calling at inconvenient hours, and letting the other person hang up first?

Do you get specific information you need, like:

Date, time, and place of appointment?

Name and position of person to whom you are talking?

Details of the conversation?

18

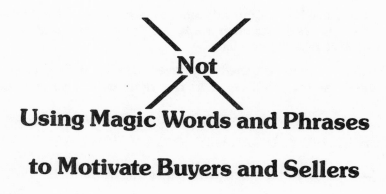

Using Magic Words and Phrases

to Motivate Buyers and Sellers

According to the dictionary, the word *magic* is defined as "something that casts a spell; an extraordinary power of influence seemingly from a supernatural source."

Wouldn't you like to use words to cast a spell, words which would have an extraordinary power of influence over your buyers and sellers? Well, you can. The words you can use to cast such a spell are not long, difficult, or unusual; they are short, simple, everyday words. Yet, surprisingly enough, these commonplace words seem to have the power to move mountains. They literally perform miracles of selling.

THE BENEFITS YOU'LL GAIN

1. You'll make friends and influence buyers, sellers, and others.
2. You'll express your ideas effectively in speech or in writing.
3. You'll control conversations and direct the course of interviews.
4. You'll encourage positive responses.

5. You'll extract important information from your prospects about themselves—what they want, need, think, and feel.

6. You'll be able to check the buying pulse of your prospects.

7. You'll paint pretty pictures to attract and excite buyers.

8. You'll exert an extraordinary power of influence over buyers and sellers.

9. Thus, you'll create and hold more interest, open more minds, and close more sales. In other words, you'll perform in a way that will achieve miracles of selling.

You can gain these benefits by developing the skill of using the right word, at the right time, in the right way, with the right prospect.

TECHNIQUES YOU CAN USE TO GAIN THESE BENEFITS

"You"—a three-letter word with powerful impact

Henry Ford once said, "If there is any one secret of success it lies in the ability to get the other person's point of view and see things from his angle as well as from your own." This may sound simple and obvious, but, surprisingly enough, 90 percent of real estate salespeople ignore it, 90 percent of the time. The other 10 percent are the "pros." They follow this guideline 100 percent of the time.

The one little word you can use to get the other person's view is *you.* Since *I* is the smallest word in the dictionary, why make it the largest word in your vocabulary? Just as repeating a person's name feeds a person's ego, so does the frequent use of the word *you.* And, when you ask a buyer or seller what he thinks, he is proud to show off his knowledge or air his thoughts. This plays powerfully upon his ego, and you'll soon find that he'll be arguing your case as though it were his own.

If you set yourself up as a counselor, offering your own opinions, you'll soon find yourself working the word *I* to the death of your sale: "*I* think this is the right house for you; *I* feel you'd be happy with this arrangement." "This is a fair offer; *I* think you should take it." "*I* don't think you should accept this offer." If, however, you ask for your prospect's opinion, you will be much more effective: "How do *you* feel about this house?" "Do *you* consider this a fair price?" "From what *you* have told me, don't *you* agree that *you* could be happy here?" "What do *you* think of this offer?" Your client may surprise you by agreeing. But even if he doesn't, you'll know how *he* views the offer.

When you use such expressions as, "*You* mentioned that ... ," "What do *you* think of ... ," "From what *you* have said ... ," "*You* indicated that ... ," you are using the secret weapon of empathy to the best advantage.

In all instances, the trick is to maximize the word *you* and minimize the word *I.* This may take a bit of practice until it becomes automatic. But when it does, you'll capture your prospect's attention, hold his interest, and perform great feats of selling.

"Why"—another little word with plenty of power

One of the most powerful words any real estate salesperson can use is the word *why.* There is no other single word quite as effective in closing a sale. When you ask "Why?" it forces an answer, some sort of commitment, a reason that is preventing your prospect from going ahead to buy or sell.

"Mr. and Mrs. Prospect, *why* do you hesitate?" forces them to give you a reason for their unwillingness to go ahead. Or, they may simply say, "I guess we really should go ahead." As you can see, asking "Why?" is an easy, direct, and effective method of asking for the order.

As a trial close, it often works well to ask, "Why not? ... Why not go back and take one more look? Then you can tell better how you feel about it." If they do, then you know they're interested. This question serves as a good indicator, especially when people are viewing a house for the first time.

Another effective way to use this little word is to clarify a particular question. A prospect may ask a simple question such as, "How close is the expressway?" The prospect could be asking this for a variety of reasons. He might want to have easy access to an expressway, or he might be concerned about the noise of traffic whizzing by, or he might be asking just out of curiosity. Rather than assuming or guessing, you can find out for sure by asking, "Why do you ask, Mr. Prospect?" His response will determine how you handle his question.

Using "when," not "if," for positive results

When you say, "If you buy this house," or, "If you decide to employ me as your agent," it implies some doubts as to whether they will or they won't. Instead, try saying, "When you live in this house," or, "When you employ me as your agent." Such a remark assumes that your prospect will buy the house or sign the listing. The next time your prospect shows interest in a particular house, or a seller is considering you as his agent, try saying "when," not "if," and you'll see how effective this can be.

When the sale falters, try the fantastic F's:
Feel, Felt, and Found

Three little words, *feel, felt,* and *found,* can do wonders at the point in the sale when your clients show a great deal of interest, yet need a little shove to make the final decision. This is how it works:

"Mr. and Mrs. Buyer, I understand how you *feel.* You still have some doubts about whether you'll be making the right decision, isn't that so? I'd like to tell you about another young couple, about your age, who *felt* the same way. They had seen a house they liked very much, but like you, it was their first house and they weren't quite sure. After weighing all the pros and cons, they decided to go ahead. They *found* that it was a great relief when they made that decision and, to show how happy it made them, they wrote this letter to tell me so. Here's the letter and here's a picture of the house they bought."

You can also use this principle in reverse. Tell them about someone who didn't go ahead, who delayed in making a decision and was sorry later. The consequences you relate can include how they lost the house because someone else bought it, or that they had to pay more later on because the price went up or interest rates increased. Of course, your example must be true. For a greater impact, produce some valid evidence.

You will note that whenever you tell your prospects about a similar situation, they will find it easy to identify with the incident. This results in quick action.

Some short, simple words to involve buyers and sellers

Although the words *how, what, where, when, which, why* and *who* are short, simple words, they do play a powerful and diversified role in selling real estate.

Begin a question with *how, what, where, when, which, why* or *who,* and you can draw out a specific response, get the other person involved, encourage him to explain and elaborate on his objectives and problems, his wants and needs, and stimulate him to think about your ideas or the service you are offering.

- *"How* many bedrooms do you need?"
- *"What* do you think of ... ?"
- *"Where* would be the most convenient location for you?"
- *"When* do you plan to give occupancy?"
- *"Which* house do you prefer, the first or the last house?"
- *"Why* are you concerned?"
- *"Who* else will be involved in making a decision?"

These little words can also be used to clarify statements or to feed back what you understood was said.

- "Is this *how* you would like to take title?"
- "Does it make a difference to you *what* date they choose to close, the 15th or the 30th?"
- "Let's put down on paper the reasons *why* you may want to buy this house, along with the reasons *why* you may not want to buy it."
- "Did you say you wanted me to find out *who* is building next door?"

In addition, you can use these same words to get a positive or negative response. This technique can start a conversation easily, confirm some specific facts, get a commitment, or reinforce previous statements.

- "Is a colonial style *what* you prefer?"
- "This is *where* you want to be located, isn't it?"
- *"Which* house did you want me to check on the taxes? It was the one on Main Street, wasn't it?"
- "You did say your father is the one *who* will co-sign, didn't you?"
- *"How* would you like the same style house but with another bedroom?"
- "Is this *why* you wanted to wait to use professional help?"

Since these three- and four-letter words can be used in so many ways, why not sprinkle them freely throughout your everyday interviews? You'll be pleased with the results.

How to put a hook into your ad

The quicker you sell your listing, the sooner you will get paid. That's what successful selling is all about. One quick way to do this is to grab the reader's attention immediately with a "hook" in the headings of your ads and brochures.

David Stone, author of the book, *Training Manual for Real Estate Salesmen,* has this to say about preparing ad headings:*

> *Every day new buyers enter the real estate market in your area. These will be people with different interests who can be classified in broad categories, based on motivational needs. By choosing your advertising copy very carefully, you can appeal to each of these groups with different ads. One can be designed to attract the "prestige" buyer while a different property is aimed at the "easy terms" buyer. To assist you in preparing good ads for the basic housing groups you serve, I have listed the following topics as major themes and given you a few suggested "ad headers" to go with them. Study these and then insert more good ad headers, or lead lines which will accent the emotional drives of the readers to whom you are trying to appeal.*

Here are some basic residential motivation categories, as described by David Stone:

Category	Basic Motivations	Possible Headings for Ads
Animals	children	"City Farmer"
	country	"Bring Your Horse"
	farms	"Raise Chickens"
	freedom	"God's Half-Acre"
	large lots	"Paradise for Pets"
	room	"Country Living"
	rural	"Home for Horses"
Convenience	close	"Walk to Work"
	comfort	"Every Convenience"
	easy	"Pleasant to Own"

---

*From the book, *Training Manual for Real Estate Salesmen,* by David Stone. ©1965, by David Stone. Published by Prentice-Hall, Inc., Englewood Cliffs, New Jersey 07632.

Category	Basic Motivations	Possible Headings for Ads
	modern	"Modern Design"
	practical	"Wife-Saver Kitchen"
	time-saving	"Close to Everything"
Handyman	creative	"Creative Castle"
	earn	"Earn Your Down Payment"
	fix	"Paint and Putter"
	imagination	"Use Your Imagination"
	invest	"Elbow Grease Needed"
	repair	"Weed It and Reap"
Privacy	beauty	"Landscaped Retreat"
	freedom	"Private Paradise"
	protected	"Nestled in a Valley"
	quiet	"Restful Cottage"
	seclusion	"Peaceful Haven"
	shaded	"Under the Pines"
Recreation	fishing	"Your Own Stream"
	hiking	"Mountain Villa"
	hunting	"Sportsman's Hideout"
	golf	"Two Golf Courses"
	playing	"Tennis Greens"
	swimming	"Cool Pool"
Tradition	architecture	"Classic Beauty"
	beauty	"Decorator's Delight"
	creative	"Restorable Retreat"
	graciousness	"Elegant Age"
	mellowed	"Old but Lovable"
	seasoned	"Traditional Two-Story"

The list could go on and on. Perhaps you're creative. If so, put on your thinking cap and add some of your own catchy and clever headings that will instantly impel people to read, and excite their curiosity to read on.

Paint a picture to inspire action

How satisfied are you with your ability to make the phone ring? Are your advertisements exciting? Do they arouse the reader's curiosity enough to call about seeing the house? With this foremost in mind, you can put exciting ideas into writing in the same way as you can in face-to-face conversations.

As you know, every house has some saleable features and benefits that you can accent. As the famous advertising slogan goes, "Sell the sizzle, not the steak." Aim your material at the individual whose needs or wants can be satisfied by owning this property. In other words, make it so appealing that the reader says to himself, "That sounds exactly like what I'm looking for."

Along these lines, here are a few samples:

- Complete privacy has been achieved without walls or fences.
- Location is right, price more so.
- Unique in design, low in price.
- Kitchen appliances arranged in step-saving shape.
- Offering a panoramic view from several rooms.
- Numerous facilities for entertainment, relaxation, or just getting away.
- Flexible financing and conveniences make this condo an unbeatable buy.
- The family room sports a fireplace and convenient serving bar.
- An immaculate basement with plenty of space for a recreation room.
- It's a putterer's paradise.
- All the charm and elegance of the South are embodied in this spacious four bedroom colonial.
- Throughout the recreation, garden, and lawn areas, there is a constantly changing pattern of natural beauty.
- A dramatic setting that is spellbinding.
- There's serene beauty in every room of this charming colonial home.
- Ranch-style home, paramount in every respect—truly a great buy.

If you don't already have a list of catchy, clever words and phrases that you can draw from, then start now to collect and catalog some. With such a collection on hand, you'll find it easy to select material for your ads that will paint pictures to generate power-pulling effects. Your phone will ring!

Words that quickly attracted a buyer

The house was located away from the metropolitan area. It was a scaled-down copy of a very expensive home. Yet, for some reason it wasn't moving. One Sunday, this ad appeared:

Mini Castle. Features designed for homes worth over $100,000. Three bedroom, two bath. Sliding glass doors open all major living areas to beautifully landscaped patio, round pool, cabana with shower. Great buy at only $47,500.

It sold that day!

Powerful phrases that work wonders in closing

One particularly powerful phrase that a super salesperson includes in his presentation is, "What do you think of it?" When you ask this after you have presented a piece of property or an idea, you'll discover just how magical these few words are. The trick here is to ask, "What do you think of it?" and then wait and wait and wait some more to hear the complete answer. When you do this, you will get the key to whichever door it opens—either the one that says, "Come on in, we are ready," or the other door which leads you in a different direction than where you want to go. This is a very effective closing technique when used properly.

Another closing phrase that produces startling results is used after you try to close with the word *why*. You listen to the response without commenting, and then ask, "In addition to that, isn't there something else, some other reason that makes you hesitate to go ahead right now?" These few words, *why* and *in addition to that*, compel a buyer or seller to reveal the real reason for his delay. This reason may take you by surprise. It could be something you didn't even suspect. When you can succeed in uncovering something that was previously unknown to you in this fashion, wouldn't you call that magic?

More phrases to perk up the ears of your buyers and sellers

Start your sentence with any of the following:

- "Here's an idea ... "
- "May I suggest ... "
- "Let's see how ... "
- "Supposing I can ... "

- "You indicated that ... "
- "When you ... "
- "What if ... "

These phrases pique a person's curiosity. They will want to hear more. As a result, you will have a captive audience. Such powerful phrases spell "opportunity"—a chance to sell an idea that will open the mind and close the sale.

How to avoid words that turn off buyers and sellers

Most people don't like to feel that they are being "sold." They much prefer to think that they are buying. You may not be aware that some of the words commonly used in selling real estate do make you sound like a salesperson. These words can often cause resistance. Both buyers and sellers alike may resent them. You can avoid using them when another word or two might be more acceptable.

Instead of:	Say:
list	employ me as your agent, act as your agent
listing	employment agreement
contract	agreement
commission	fee, brokerage fee
down payment	initial investment
monthly payment	monthly investments
total price or cost	total investment
sign	endorse, authorize, approve, write your name exactly as it appears on the top of the page
price reduction	price adjustment
deal	transaction, opportunity
you don't understand	perhaps I didn't make myself clear
yes, but	I know how you feel, what do you think of this idea? I see what you mean, tell me, have you thought about ...

Using magic words to gain power over your clients

Since selling real estate involves skillful communication with various types of people, you must use the right word, at the right time, to express your ideas effectively in speaking or in writing. So, choose your words wisely and weigh them well.

When you employ the tried and tested magical words and phrases set forth in this chapter, you will appreciate how easy they are to use and how powerful they can be. No matter how often you use them, they won't go out of style. They persuade, convince, and motivate both buyers and sellers.

As you probably noticed, these words are all part of our common, everyday language. Yet, when you make them an integral part of your everyday selling conversation, you will find yourself probing for information better, solving problems faster, closing sales easier, and, therefore, exerting extraordinary influence over your customers and clients.

Checklist for Using Powerful Words and Phrases

Do you practice using plenty of "you" appeal?

> Refrain from using "I"?

> Use "you" frequently to:
> get your prospect's viewpoint?
> capture and hold your prospect's attention?

Do you realize the full impact of using "why?"

> Use "why" to close?

> Use "why" to clarify the reason behind the question?

> Use, as a final close, "Why ... In addition, isn't there something else?"

Do you get information and involve the buyer and seller by using words like the following:

> *How, what, where, which, when, why, who*?

Do you try substituting an assumptive "when" for an implied "if"?

Do you help your buyers and sellers to arrive at a favorable decision by using the reassuring words, *"feel, felt, found"*?

Do you use power-pulling words in your advertisement?

Do you inspire action with written descriptions of your listing?

Do you include in your sales talk, as often as you can, the sales-clinching phrase, "What do you think of it?"

Do you pique the curiosity of your buyer or seller with:

    Here's an idea?

    May I suggest?

    Let's see how?

    Supposing I can?

    You indicate that?

    When you?

    What if?

Do you avoid using certain words that turn off the buyer or seller?

19

Failure to
Spot and Heed "Buy" Signals

As its name connotes, a "buy signal" is a signal sent to express, indicate, or signify a desire to buy. In selling real estate, this signal is transmitted by something a buyer says or does which conveys the message that he sees himself as the owner, living in the house. Or, in the case of a seller, he visualizes his house as sold, enabling him to leave it.

You can compare this type of signal to the signs that appear along the highways. The road signs are there for your benefit, to caution you or convey helpful information and directions. Some signs are warnings such as, "Detour—Bridge Washed Out," "Sharp Curve Ahead," or "Slippery When Wet." That kind of sign calls your attention to hazards ahead and notifies you to proceed carefully and cautiously. Other signs give you specific directions and information, such as, "Next Exit ½ Mile," "Left Lane to Route 6," "Take Right Lane to Kalamazoo." If you don't pay attention to the signs, you can miss the turnoff that leads to where you are going. In fact, you might not be able to get back on the road for some time. And, if you should continue in the wrong direction, you won't get to your destination at all.

The same ideas apply when you travel along the highways of a real estate selling career. You will encounter signs for your benefit. Some will be warnings and some will convey information and directions. It does not much matter whether these signals are flashed orally or expressed by actions. What does matter is that you spot them and heed them.

THE BENEFITS YOU'LL GAIN

1. You'll be aware, alert, and attuned to signs that signify that your prospect is ready to move ahead.
2. You'll receive reliable clues regarding whatever you are offering, an idea, a piece of property, or a listing service.
3. You won't waste time going in the wrong direction.
4. You won't bypass the signals which lead you directly to your goal.
5. You'll perceive and pay attention to affirmations and confirmations.
6. You won't take the trip in vain.
7. You'll arrive safely and quickly at your destination—a sale.
8. You'll make your buyers and sellers happy because you will have helped them to solve their problems.
9. You'll become proficient at closing more sales.
10. You'll shorten your journey to a successful selling career.

TECHNIQUES YOU CAN USE TO GAIN THESE BENEFITS

Noticing "buy" signals

Before you can spot a "buy" signal, it is helpful to be aware that the signs you are looking for can be transmitted either with words (what they say), or with gestures (what they do). In addition, such signs can appear frequently and in different places during your presentation. Knowing this, you can see how important it is for you to train yourself to be on guard at all times, constantly watching and waiting, always alert and ready to take action at any given moment.

Few prospects will tell you outright that they are ready to buy, or that they want your service. Yet, they do reveal what is going on inside their minds through various telltale signs.

Good closers know that certain words, facial expressions, and actions can be conclusive clues that their prospects are convinced or ready to perform. Therefore, being "tuned in" to what is happening around them, they are able to capitalize on these signals, thereby making more sales or getting more listings.

You can begin to train yourself to do this by learning to listen with your eyes, as well as with your ears, for *any* and *all* messages that seem to say, "I'm interested, I'm ready to go ahead." The more you practice the art of watchful listening, the easier it will become to spot these signals, and the more proficient you will become in using them advantageously to close a sale or listing.

Comments buyers make which signify interest

Although buyers generally do not tell you in so many words that they want to buy whatever you are offering, they do signify their interest with certain comments. Such comments constitute the "buy" signals which notify you that they, the buyers, see themselves as the owners, living in the house.

Here are some typical remarks which demonstrate this:

- "John, I wonder if our dining room furniture will fit into this room?"
- "Which room would we give to Mary and which to Manny?"
- "With this fenced yard, I wouldn't have to worry about the two little ones. They could play outdoors by themselves."
- "This would be ideal as a sewing room for me."
- "This traffic-free plan would sure make it easier to keep the rest of the house tidy."
- "I wonder if we could be in before school opens?"
- "How close is a shopping center?"
- "Can we really use this wood-burning fireplace?"
- "I didn't notice; let's check to see if there are adequate electrical outlets in all the rooms."
- "Will these air-conditioner units really be enough to make it comfortable in the summer?"
- "The drapes in this room are unusually attractive; will they remain?"

Comments such as these are really saying, "We are interested." That being the case, you should watch for them.

Listening for more "go" signs

When a person is thinking seriously about buying the property, he notifies you of his intent by making inquiries or statements concerning the details about the price, mortgage, taxes, date of occupancy, or items included:

- "How long does it take to get a loan application approved?"
- "If we were to put 20 percent down, what would our monthly payments be?"
- "How much would go for immediate expenses?"
- "I think it is overpriced. I don't think it's worth $72,000."
- "What do you think the seller will take? Is the seller firm on his price?"
- "We like those wall brackets and bookcases in the library. Would they be included?"
- "Does the solar heating system really supply enough hot water all the time?"
- "We must be in before school starts. Is that possible?"
- "How much did you say the taxes are?"
- "Is the present mortgage assumable? Do you think the seller would consider a small second mortgage?"
- "Will the seller consider selling VA?"

These are questions that a salesperson often looks upon as routine information. In reality, the customer is asking because he is interested and is thinking of buying. When you recognize them as definite "buy" signs, you can treat them as such and follow through to close more sales.

A $45,000 sale in a half-hour

A call came in on an ad that had been placed in a real estate magazine. In addition to the picture and the usual basic information, the ad carried the address and the price of the house. When Mr. K. called, he said that he and his wife were down the highway heading toward the neighborhood and would like to be met at the location in 15 minutes.

As they went through the house, they talked freely. Mr. K. mentioned that he was a teacher in a nearby boys' school and that he wanted to ride to school on his bicycle. Of the three bedrooms, they commented that one bedroom would be used as his study, while a second bedroom seemed just right for Mrs. K. to work on her ceramics. When they arrived at the carport, Mrs. K. noticed that there was 220 wiring, which would be adequate power for operating her kiln. Yet, despite all these buying signals that were flashing away, they were beginning to show some of the typical signs of hesitating.

I asked, "Mr. and Mrs. K., what financial arrangements were you planning on in purchasing your home?" The answer was the clincher.

It was their second marriage. Mrs. K. had sold her house, the proceeds of which they planned to invest in the purchase of their new home. Of the total amount, they were willing to initially invest $15,000, with the balance in cash at closing. A brief summary of their own comments reinforced their feelings. They agreed that this house had everything they were looking for, including the right price for them, and they readily consented to purchase it at once.

This was an easy, quick sale. What made it so was spotting the various strong "buy" signals and immediately acting on them.

- The location was perfect. The house was close enough for Mr. K. to be able to ride a bike to school.
- One room was right for a study to hold Mr. K.'s books.
- Another room was an ideal work room for Mrs. K.
- Having adequate wiring for Mrs. K.'s kiln already installed was a bonus.
- The price was acceptable.
- Financing was no problem.

Although this may seem like an oversimplification of the selling process, it really isn't. Each time you are with a prospect, if you really listen, you, too, will spot the buying signals and, if you are alert, you won't pass them by. Instead, you'll take advantage and make the sale quickly.

Signals sellers flash

Like the buyers, most sellers do not come right out and say in specific words that they are ready to buy—that is, to buy your service or to accept the offer you are presenting. Usually, they won't say, "I want to list my house with you," or, "Yes, I'll accept this offer." But what they will do to signify this intention is flash signals by asking certain questions or making particular statements:

- "How long would it take to get the house on Multiple Listing?"
- "Would you hold the house open every Sunday?"
- "You can set any price you want, but I want $75,000 for myself."
- "If we were to give you this listing, how do I know you will do all the things you said you would?"
- "How much do you think you could sell this house for?"
- "If we accept this price of $72,000, how much would we have left after our expenses are taken out?"
- "What difference does it make if we list with you or with XYZ company? You're both on Multiple Listing, aren't you?"
- "I would like to see what price you arrive at."
- "I like the idea of promising to keep a seller informed of what's going on."

These few examples demonstrate that, even though he hasn't actually said so, the seller is thinking of you as his agent to sell his house. This is the type of sign you should be on the lookout for.

Observing the positive signs of body language

Little things a person does can tell you many things that their lips won't. Without words, their actions can express their interest and their feelings:

- Picking up the brochure or the contract indicates, "I want to take a closer look. I want to check on some of the details."
- Nodding up and down says, "I do understand. Yes, I agree with what you are telling me. Yes, that is so."
- A pleasant smile means, "I like that. It pleases me. That's a good idea."
- Lingering in a room: "I want to take it all in, and not overlook anything. I think this room fits into our plans so I'll take my time and look closely to be sure that it does."
- Going back into a room or through the whole house: "This has possibilities. I like it. I want to make doubly sure."
- Whispering to each other: "What do you think? I like it, do you? What do you think we should do about it? How much shall we offer?"
- Making notes: "I don't want to rely on my memory. I'll jot down details of what impresses me about this house."

- Figuring on paper: "I need to do some figuring to see how we could work it out. Let's see what it would come to if we paid X number of dollars. How much of a second mortgage should we try to ask the owner to take back? What different ways could we handle the financing?"

Look for nonverbal clues that indicate a positive attitude. They'll affect your attitude, too, leading you positively toward closing more sales.

Noticing negative signs

When you are checking the pulse of your buyer or seller, it is equally important to notice the negative signs as well as the positive signs. These signs tell you that they aren't interested, so you'd better change your tactics:

- Frowning indicates: "I don't quite understand. Please explain. I'm confused."
- Shaking head from side to side: "No, no! I don't agree. I don't like it."
- Sitting back, up straight, perhaps with folded hands, says, "Show me. You've got to prove it."
- Yawning: "I'm bored. I'm too tired to pay attention."
- Looking at watch: "This is taking too long. I'm not interested. Let's move on. I must get out of here."
- Raising an eyebrow: "I'm not so sure that's so."
- Looking off in the distance: "You've just lost me."
- Doodling: "I'm indifferent to what you are telling me."
- Peering over the tops of glasses: "I don't believe what you're telling me."
- Quickly removing eyeglasses and tossing them on the table: "I don't like this at all. You've gone too far."
- Clearing throat: "That's not the way I see it. You listen to me. Now, here's the way I look at it."

Being alert and properly reading both the favorable and unfavorable messages transmitted by body language can help you to determine how soon and how safely you will arrive at your destination of closing the sale. Be on guard and enjoy productive sales relationships with your buyers and sellers.

Watch out for objections—they can be buying signals

Star real estate salespeople will tell you that the hardest person to sell is the one with a poker face, the one who remains silent and expressionless throughout your presentation. Without a doubt, that kind of prospect is the most difficult to close because you never know what he thinks or where you stand. On the other hand, the one who procrastinates and seems to voice objections is often the easiest person to close because, on the surface, what appears to be an objection is often a positive sign.

A buyer or seller might say, "I want to sleep on it," "I really should wait," "I'd like to check," "We want to think it over," "We'll call you tomorrow morning," or "Thank you for all your trouble, but we really want to talk it over some more."

Or a seller may say, "We want to try it ourselves for a little longer," "After the last experience we had, no thank you," "We wouldn't want to go through that again," "You Realtors are all alike, you're on our doorstep all the time until you get the listing; then you disappear and forget all about us," or "If we don't give any one broker the listing, then anyone can sell it and earn a commission. I think we'll get more action that way and we won't be tied up to just one broker for any length of time."

What they are really saying is, "We are interested, but we're not ready yet, we're fearful about making the wrong decision, and *we need more convincing.* Please help us! Tell us why we should do this now, rather than later on or perhaps not at all."

Once you realize that remarks like these are pleas for help, not rejections, then you'll look upon them as positive "buy" signs rather than negative ones and you'll be sure to treat them that way.

Making the most of telltale signs

Whenever you receive a positive signal, you should take advantage and try for a close. Whenever you receive a negative signal, you should change your course. But, surprisingly enough, these "buy" signs go unnoticed all too often. The salesperson is often sleeping at the switch, thus he goes on and on and oversells.

However, if you recognize the buying signals, and if you are alert and watching for them, you won't let one slip by without taking the appropriate action for trying to close right then and there.

You can vary your actions according to the particular signal. For instance, when your prospect picks up a brochure or a contract and studies it, give him all the time he needs to digest every word. Wait until he finishes, and then listen very closely to the favorable remarks he makes or the way he discusses it. If, however, he puts the papers down without comment, then you can use the effective closing question, "What do you think?"

The bottom line

Any favorable sign may serve as a cue to attempt to close. In his book, *Secrets of Closing Sales,* Charles B. Roth, who is a well-known master salesman, sales trainer, and counselor, had this to say about the importance of making the close fast:*

> And one form of your alertness must be that you must never, never try to talk after you have decided the buyer is ready for the close. If you do, you'll lose sales. The important thing to remember in good closing is to close just as soon as you can, and not permit any sale to drag on one second longer than is necessary. Even if you have delivered only half your sales talk and made only a few of your sales points; even if you feel you have not advanced your strongest arguments in favor of your goods or services, if you get any hint that indicates the close is at hand, drop everything, stop talking, step in and try to close.

So, follow the guidelines set forth in this chapter, and you'll master the skill in spotting "buy" signals. Be determined to heed each and every one of them and you'll find yourself among the best closers—the top producers.

Checklist for Perceiving "Buy" Signals

Do you treat the committing comments the buyer and seller make as closing cues:

Owner remarks indicating he saw the house as "sold"?

Prospect's remarks indicating he saw his family living in the house?

Do you attempt to close in response to their questions which signify interest in performing, as when:

Buyer asks about mortgage, occupancy date, price, terms?

---

*From the book, *Secrets of Closing Sales,* by Charles B. Roth. ©1970, by Prentice-Hall, Inc. Published by Prentice-Hall, Inc., Englewood Cliffs, New Jersey 07632.

Seller asks about price, Multiple Listing, special services, open house?

Do you listen to the buyer and the seller with your eyes as well as your ears?

Observe their telltale body movements?

Heed positive signs such as:
Picking up brochure or contract?
Nodding up and down?
Smiling pleasantly?
Lingering in a room?
Going back into a room or through the whole house again?
Whispering to each other?
Making notes?
Figuring on paper?

Notice negative signs such as:
Frowning?
Shaking head from side to side?
Sitting back, straightening up, with folded arms?
Yawning?
Looking at watch?
Raising an eyebrow?
Looking off in the distance?
Doodling?
Peering over the tops of glasses?
Quickly removing glasses and tossing them on the table?
Clearing throat?

Do you feel you were on the alert for objections that could be turned into reasons to buy now?

Do you always try to close immediately after each "buy" sign?

20

Neglecting to

Reach Out for Growth and More Profit

Today, opportunities for a successful selling career in real estate are truly limitless. Probably no one is more aware of this than the broker who has witnessed how rapidly the industry has grown and expanded in the past 10 to 15 years. Yet, in spite of this continued enormous growth and great opportunities, many real estate salespeople are not making the most of their profession or of their personal potential.

As a real estate agent, you may have years of experience, yet you may not reach your full potential or reap the available rich rewards if you neglect to take some steps to check up on your selling effectiveness at regular intervals. No matter how busy you find yourself with hectic daily activities, you'll discover that the key to fulfillment is to stop and devote some time to reflecting on where you've been in your real estate career and where you are going.

Since the real estate profession is frequently referred to as a "business of numbers," the first step to think about is calculating the numbers: the number of calls it takes to get an appointment, the number of interviews it takes to get a listing, the number of prospects it takes to get a sale. With only so many working hours in a day, the road to success is paved by decreasing the number of attempts it takes in each situation to get results.

That is precisely what this book is designed to do. The guidelines presented, if they are followed, will improve your selling effectiveness. In other words, they will help you to work smarter, not necessarily harder. The mistakes mentioned in this book are the most common major mistakes being made today, particularly by many agents who have been active in the field for some time. During this time, they have unwittingly developed some poor selling habits. By following the specific tested and proven techniques suggested here, you can learn new solutions to old problems. Of equal importance, you can also be helped to "unlearn" some of the things you have been doing wrong, so that you can correct whatever costly mistakes you may be making.

This final chapter shows you how you can increase your earnings and make the most of your ability by giving yourself a sales-saver checkup, by evaluating the effectiveness of your efforts, by finding new profitable ideas, by capitalizing on entering into an area of specialization, and more.

THE BENEFITS YOU'LL GAIN

1. You'll constantly upgrade your selling skills and step up your effectiveness.
2. You'll improve yourself today and make yourself better for tomorrow.
3. You'll avoid standing still. You'll go forward.
4. You'll value your victories. They'll serve as a stimulus for further successful sessions.
5. You'll eliminate your weaknesses. You'll search for preventive measures, and you'll correct your mistakes before they spell failure.
6. You'll seek new approaches to old problems. You'll change with the changing times.
7. You'll analyze and actionize. You'll determine what went wrong, where and when. You'll know what works and what doesn't.
8. You'll enjoy good mental health. You'll learn to cope with stress in a crisis and rid yourself of fear and frustration.
9. You'll find it easier to keep yourself enthusiastic, excited, and motivated.
10. You'll widen your horizons with greater knowledge.

11. You'll capitalize on your moneymaking time to gain peak performances.
12. You'll appreciate side effects: making more friends, reaching out to and influencing more people.
13. You'll improve your professional stature.
14. You'll become an expert. You'll keep yourself abreast of current developments in your specialty.
15. You'll prevent economic suicide.
16. You'll learn, learn, learn—grow, grow, grow—earn, earn, earn.
17. And how pleased you'll be to see your commission checks continue to increase!

Are you sufficiently satisfied with your daily performance? Do you feel that you are working at your top capacity now, or do you honestly feel that you could do better? Are there times when you'd like to rid your body of tension, stress, and frustration? Well, you now have the opportunity to develop your full potential, tap your creative processes, and enjoy the benefits of the periodic sales checkup.

TECHNIQUES YOU CAN USE TO GAIN THESE BENEFITS

Making the review a regular ritual for a better tomorrow

At the end of the day, while what transpired is still fresh in your mind, and before planning your tomorrow, you'll find it most beneficial to take a few moments to reflect and review the events of the day. Think first about what went well, recalling your successes and patting yourself on the back for the smallest, most minute success you may have had. This is important. When you endorse yourself for the things you did right, it's a great morale booster. It gives you confidence to go forward to meet the challenges ahead.

Next, ask yourself what went wrong. Then, step by step, review and replay the events in your mind. Soon, a light will probably go on in your head, and you'll see clearly what happened and what you could have done differently. When this hits you, you'll wonder why you didn't realize it at the time, since it is so obvious now. This is a normal, common reaction.

Once you discover the mistake, the next step is to determine if and how you can rectify it. Thus, you'll be excited about trying out the solution tomorrow.

If, however, the error seems completely beyond repair, chalk it up to experience, profit by it, and resolve not to let it happen again.

A realistic approach to assessing your performance

It is very easy to blame somebody or something for your present problems. A salesperson may often be heard to say, "They're not dependable. They don't know what they want. They're too stubborn," or, "It's too wet or cold. No one will be out. It's holiday time. It's a buyer's market. It's a seller's market. Mortgage money's too tight, so why waste time contacting buyers or sellers now?" or, "This house will never sell; it's too high priced, too old, too dilapidated, or the seller's too difficult." The excuses go on and on. It's always someone else's fault for not making the sale or getting the listing. It is easy to try to justify your woes with such thoughts, but if you want to succeed, here are some suggestions to guide you in realistically assessing your performance. When you evaluate yourself:

- *Be totally honest.* If you lie to yourself, you only fool yourself.
- *Distinguish the difference between fact and fancy.* Face the facts as they really are and not as you wish them to be. Optimism is healthy, but too much optimism can be misleading and can even prove fatal.
- *Admit your mistakes.* Rather than rationalize away your errors, acknowledge them.
- *Assume responsibility for your own actions.* Have the courage to blame no one else but yourself for whatever goes wrong.

With this approach in mind, you can see the problem as it really is, pinpoint your mistakes, and be in a position to find a remedy. In the process, you'll probably discover that self-awareness can be a profitable tool.

Checking your pulse rate to see how fast you are going

It is true that medicine is not an exact science. Neither is selling real estate. Yet, it is surprising how your selling effectiveness can be measured by studying your records and how the findings foretell your future potential.

The doctor checks your pulse rate to see how fast your heart is going. You can take the pulse rate of your sales so you can see how fast *you* are going.

Usually, the daily review will reveal the present condition of your performance, enabling you to detect early signs of any problems that might be brewing and to take some preventive measures. However, it is from the total picture at the end of the week or the month that you can determine the results of your efforts.

First, carefully examine and evaluate these records, the number of calls you made, the interviews you had, and the results. Then, carefully study the findings so that you can see where you are going and at what rate. Now you can determine the course of action you feel would be most beneficial. Perhaps you will find that you are being consistent in your production. In this case, you will, no doubt, decide to continue doing the same things in the same way. If, however, you find that you need to concentrate on improving particular areas, such as making appointments, obtaining listings, closing sales, or even getting referrals, you can plan the steps you want to take to bring better results.

If your selling pulse rate seems to be satisfactory, continue with the same procedures; but, if you should discover signs of regressing or failing, determine what changes might alter your course and then try them.

How to change with the changing times

Many real estate salespeople are fearful of change. They find it more comfortable doing things in a certain way, the same way they have always done them. They resist change.

In his book, *The 22 Biggest Mistakes Managers Make and How to Correct Them,* James K. Van Fleet says not to accept the present system as the best or only way. He believes that "change always starts with an idea." He presents "some methods that Chris Ireland, Director of Dow Chemical's Special Projects Division, says you can use to change the status quo and revamp your present system so you can go for the maximum":*

Re-examine your thinking. *Repress old ideas and solutions; push the accepted methods aside temporarily while you look for new methods. Examine new ideas with the uninhibited curiosity*

---

*From the book, *The 22 Biggest Mistakes Managers Make and How to Correct Them,* by James K. Van Fleet. ©1973, by Parker Publishing Company, Inc. Published by Parker Publishing Company, Inc., West Nyack, New York 10994.

of a child. Develop the knack of seeing things as if you were seeing them for the very first time.

Do some brainstorming with other people. *Probe the minds of others. Use questions to stimulate thinking. The method here is to suspect critical judgment while suggesting new ideas. There's plenty of time for evaluation later. Now you want as many new ideas as possible. So no matter how crazy a method sounds, jot it down. You must create a free-wheeling atmosphere to get the most out of brainstorming.*

Keep your imagination turned on all the time. *Don't turn your brain off when you go home from work. Fresh ideas can pop up all the time, during conversation with a friend—while reading a magazine or newspaper—walking, shaving, showering, eating. You can force your mind to work all the time if you will. Keep a notebook handy. You never know when that idea is going to come and you don't want to miss it.*

Be willing to accept new ideas. *It's easy to come up with all sorts of reasons why something new won't work. If you want your people to do their best to come up with new ideas and ways of doing things, then you must keep an open mind. You must be willing to give their ideas a fair try.*

Therefore, if you want to progress in today's complex real estate market, and if you don't choose to go stale, stand still, or even go backwards, then keep thinking, seeking, and trying new ideas.

A selling secret—maximize your successes, minimize your failures

It is not at all uncommon for a salesperson to dwell on his or her shortcomings, disappointments, and failures. There's a natural tendency to do this, but it can be devastating, so don't let it happen to you.

Instead, use this selling secret of super salespeople: *Accent the positive, not the negative.* Savor the successes, no matter how small they seem. Keep dwelling on them. On the other hand, don't dwell on the failures, no matter how big they may be.

When you cease dwelling on the setbacks, you will dispel feelings of depression, defeat, or discouragement. In addition, when you value your victories and when you keep on endorsing yourself for your achievements, you will be mentally prepared to tackle the rebuffs, to take a loss and turn it into a win. By doing so, you'll go forward with greater confidence, determination, and enthusiasm.

Maximize your successes and minimize your failures. You'll surely gain in mental health while you're making success a habit.

Seven ways to overcome the slump in selling real estate

In selling real estate, you will find yourself hitting peaks and valleys. There are days when you think you're on top of the world, excited with a feeling that nothing can stop you now, while on other days you feel so low, so discouraged, that everything seems to go wrong. At such times, you may find yourself blaming others: It's all their fault, buyers are not dependable, sellers can't be trusted, money's too tight, it's a seller's market, so what's the use?

You're in a slump and it's easy to be consumed by such feelings. You can, however, prepare yourself mentally to combat these negative thoughts and feelings. The best answer I found is to *do something. Take some positive action.* Here are seven easy ways to turn you "on" again:

1. Work harder, with a more determined attitude. Even though your first impulse is to withdraw, don't. Once you accept the challenge, you'll get caught up in the momentum, thinking of new things to do or new approaches to what you have been doing. As you get involved, you'll begin to feel better about everyone and everything.

2. Call, chat with, and check up on former customers and clients. Find out what's been happening to them or their neighbors. You may be pleasantly surprised by ending up with some referrals or interesting leads.

3. Change your pace. If you've been working on showing properties, try going out for listings; or work in a new area or a different field. Instead of homes, try condos, townhouses, or perhaps a different price range. As you change your interests, so will your thoughts change. It has a refreshing effect.

4. Have lunch or dinner with other successful associates who think positively. You'll be amazed at how contagious enthusiasm can be. Before long, you too will be radiating enthusiasm.

5. Attend lectures and seminars, or take a course. Generally, you'll find them stimulating and motivating. One new idea may spark your interest and you'll be eager to get going. Or, you may be reminded of some successful things you used to do that you have either forgotten or unintentionally discarded.

6. Remind yourself that, although setbacks are disturbing, you know they aren't fatal. If you realize this, you will begin to act positively and constructively.

7. Think optimistically. Remember what Winston Churchill once said: "An *optimist* sees an opportunity in every calamity; a *pessimist* sees a calamity in every opportunity."

How optimism saved the sale

This story is an example of the difference attitude can make.

George, an experienced broker, submitted a fine contract on one of my listings. The buyers both had good government jobs. They planned on a 70 percent mortgage, investing $15,000, and applying for a $30,000 loan on the purchase of the $45,000 house. Of course, the contract was immediately accepted by the very anxious sellers. This was on a Friday.

That Monday morning, George called, and he was very upset. The sale could not be consummated. Over the weekend, he had been out looking at open houses. Several salespeople he had talked to told him that their sales were going down the drain because of the money crunch. They told him that the tight money market was terrible, and that there was absolutely no money available for loans. And they were right. After a couple of calls to Savings and Loan companies, George was convinced that there was no money for loans and so he thought his sale would be lost, too.

Surely, I thought, someone must have some money. This was too good a sale to lose. We must exhaust all possibilities before giving up. I was sure we could get it somewhere. So, I offered to shop around further to see if I could locate one lending institution who would be willing to handle this small but good mortgage.

To the first few calls I got the same response as George had received. They were sorry, they did appreciate our past business, but they just didn't have any money at that time. Undaunted, determined, and still optimistic, I continued making calls. On the fourth call, I reached a loan officer who said, "Yes, we do have money. Bring your people in today and we'll be happy to take care of them." George was amazed. He was so convinced that it was hopeless that he had given up after the first few calls.

Here's the interesting part of the story. George hadn't even bothered to contact this particular Savings and Loan. When I told him the name of the lender that would be handling the mortgage, George laughed. It turned out to be the very Savings and Loan where he did his own personal business. He had been ready from the start to write the sale off as "lost" because of the tight money market. George almost lost the sale because he was not determined to succeed.

How to sharpen your selling skills and grow

Even if you have been selling real estate for 20 or 30 years, you should still be looking for new ideas, more knowledge, facts, and information. After all, growth is truly the heart of salesmanship. There are various steps you can take to strengthen your weaknesses and sharpen your selling skills, so that you can keep growing.

Initially, a review of this book might motivate you and act as a stimulus to read other books for further inspiration and knowledge.

Then you might make a concerted effort to attend seminars and lectures, take courses, and listen to tapes. Many of these are available through your local real estate boards. Others may be obtained from nearby colleges and universities. When you take advantage and make use of all available resources, you're bound to find ways to overcome your weaknesses, thus strengthening your selling skills. In a nutshell, when you learn, you'll grow, and you'll see how much more you can earn.

How a "pro" earned a $50,000 commission
with one new idea

At a Board of Realtors' Commercial-Investment Seminar, Realtor Gary S. was discussing the importance of continuous education for real estate salespeople. He testified to the fact that after he had completed one particular course, he was able to apply one idea which earned for him $50,000.

It seems that Gary had been working with a client for a few years, trying to get him to sell his 65 acres, but he could not get him to budge. When Gary learned about tax deferred exchange, he realized that this could be the answer. This principal was explained to the seller, and then to his attorney and his accountant. All of them agreed that it was a good idea.

Thus, the sale was consummated, and Gary earned his commission of $50,000.

You can see how just one new idea can help to maximize your moneymaking time. No doubt, real estate salespeople throughout the country can submit testimonials of the business generated as the result of an idea learned at some educational program. Why not join them?

Widen your horizons with beneficial side effects

Whenever you attend a seminar or take a course, in addition to the opportunity of acquiring knowledge that you can turn into profitable dollars, you will notice additional benefits, some pleasant side effects.

The change of pace proves to be healthy. You can relax a bit and free your mind from any pressing problems. When you return to work, you'll feel refreshed, with renewed spirit and enthusiasm.

Some of the people you have a chance to chat with are often interesting, while others may develop into valuable contacts for the future. Sometimes it's pleasant just to renew acquaintances with salespeople you haven't seen for a while.

There's always the possibility of sharing information on your listings or running into someone who has just what you are looking for to show to your "hot" prospect.

If you are the kind of person who makes a point of attending educational sessions, you'll agree that you usually gain more than knowledge, which is your original purpose for going. You can have some fun, laughter, a good time, and make some important contacts. If nothing else, you'll usually find that you're motivated, psyched up, and raring to go again.

If you come away with just one idea, a friend, or good feelings about yourself and your career, then you can chalk up the session you have attended as a positive, profitable experience.

A worthwhile way to insure your future—specialize

During your periodic checkup you might ask yourself, "Am I maintaining my professionalism? How can I improve my sales possibilities? What can I do to insure my future?" One response to these questions is to pick a field that appeals to you and specialize in it.

You've probably noticed that real estate, like all other professions, has become complex, complicated, and computerized, with constant changes within the industry. Today, buyers and sellers are more sophisticated and knowledgeable. There was a time when a real estate agent could learn with little effort all there was to know about real estate. That no longer holds true, because we now live in an era of specialization.

In fact, there are even specialties within specialties, which gives you a wide variety to choose from. For instance, "residential" is an umbrella that encompasses other areas, such as single homes, condominiums, and duplexes. "Commercial investment" includes shopping centers, apartment buildings, office buildings, and acreage. Perhaps you might want to consider being an expert in appraising, leasing, managing, exchanging, developing, or syndicating.

Choose a particular field that appeals to you. Investigate and explore it, study and learn as much as you can about it. And when you study your chosen specialty, you will not have to do it by yourself. Real estate boards and many colleges now offer courses where you can easily acquire the knowledge and gain recognition, thereby earning specific designations on various levels.

Select a specialty, become an authority, and improve your sales possibilities. It's a great way to insure your real estate career.

Facts

It's a *fact*... Today's buyers and sellers are more sophisticated and knowledgeable.

It's a *fact*... Modern real estate is complicated, complex, and computerized.

It's a *fact*... Competition is keener than ever.

It's a *fact*... The local real estate market is bigger, more varied, and more complicated than ever before.

It's a *fact*... Laws and regulations governing zoning and taxes are constantly changing.

It's a *fact*... New and flexible financing methods are appearing regularly in the mortgage marketplace.

Conclusion

You should learn to cope with these facts so that you can feel fit financially and emotionally. You can do that if you follow the suggestions in this chapter for giving yourself a periodic sales checkup. But don't stop there. Always keep on adding more successful strategies to your list of techniques. When you do, you will enjoy a richer, fuller life. You will feel fulfilled, because you will have reached your full potential as a happy, successful, professional real estate salesperson.

Checklist for Evaluating Your Selling Effectiveness

During your periodic sales checkup, do you:

    Review the activities at the end of your day?

    Recall the positive successful activities first?

    Congratulate yourself for them?

    Replay the unsuccessful activities step by step?

    Ask yourself how you could have acted differently?

    Decide if change might have brought about success?

    Plan how you'll try out the solution the next day?

    Stay totally honest?

    See the situation accurately and not wishfully?

    Admit your mistakes?

    Assume responsibility for your actions?

At the end of each week or month, do you:

    Carefully examine and evaluate the calls you made?

    Determine the number of interviews and their results?

    Note the changes from the last period and the trend over time?

    Decide if your performance was adequate?

If the rate is unsatisfactory, do you outline ideas requiring improvement, such as:

    Making appointments?

    Obtaining listings?

    Closing sales?

    Getting referrals?

Do you change with the times by:

Reexamining your thinking and keeping your mind fresh for new ideas?

Brainstorming with other people and taking notes, restricting criticism?

Staying prepared for capturing new ideas any time, any place?

Being willing to accept and try new ideas?

Accenting and savoring the positive?

Noting what went wrong with negatives and then dismissing them?

Considering whether you could benefit by specializing and then selecting a specialty?

Do you avoid getting into a sales slump?

Work harder with a more determined attitude?

Call, chat, or check with former customers and clients for referrals?

Try a change of pace?

Seek the company of some successful sales associates who think positively?

Improve your self-image, gain new enthusiasm by attending educational or motivational lectures, seminars, or courses?

Refrain from feeling that mistakes are fatal?

Index

A

ABC rule for closing, 194
Ads:
   putting hook in, 222-223
   key rules for writing, 118
   responses from, 119
Advertising media, 117
"Alternate-choice" question, 48-49
Arguing, 41-42
Assumption special clauses, 114
Attempting closing often enough (*see*
   Closing, attempting often enough)

B

Bethlehem Steel Company, 25
Bettger, Frank, 71,72,161
Board of Realtors Multiple Listing
   agreement, 143
Buyer, right to approve, 114
"A Buyer's Quickie Qualifying
   Questionnaire," 75,77
Buying signals, 59-60, 157
"Buy" signals, spotting and heeding,
   229-238
  benefits gained, 230
  body language, 234-235
   negative, 235
   positive, 234-235
  the bottom line, 237
  checklist, 237-238
  comments made, 231
  "go" signs, 231-232
  making most of telltale signs, 236-237
  noticing, 230-231
  objections as buying signals, 236
  signals sellers flash, 233-234
  techniques used to gain benefits,
   229-237

C

Camp David, 176
"Change-the-subject" technique, 141
Checklists:
   for asking questions, 51-52
   for controlling the selling process,
    145-146
   for determining a qualified buyer or
    seller, 85-87
   for effectively servicing the listing,
    124-125
   for evaluating your selling effectiveness,
    250-251
   for executing an effective listing
    presentation, 109
   for following through, 189
   for getting offers accepted quickly,
    179-180
   handy, 28
   for increasing rate of closing, 203-204
   for listening effectively, 61-62
   for making maximum use of the
    telephone, 214-215
   for perceiving "buy" signals, 237-238
   for planning effective presentation, 97
   for planning a productive day, 22-23, 32
   for preventing overpricing of property,
    135
   for overcoming talking too much, 42
   for showing property effectively, 158-159
   for storytelling, 166-167
   for tools of the trade, 27
   for using feedback advantageously, 70
   for using powerful words and phrases,
    227-228
Chesterfield, Lord, 124
Clincher, most effective (*see* Storytelling)
Closing consciousness, 191
Closing, attempting often enough, 191-204
  asking, importance of, 202-203
  benefits gained, 192

Closing, attempting often enough *(cont'd)*
  best place for, 194-195
  changing subjects when sale founders, 197
  checklist, 203-204
  contract in full view, 199-200
  convincing with third party story, 197
  creating atmosphere of acceptance, 195
    closing question, 195
    listening to answers, 195
    repetition, 195
    using prospect's name often, 195
  handling objections to, 200-203
    consulting attorney first, 201-202
    relatives must see first, 201
  locking in the sale, 198-199
  more ways to close, 199
  offering a choice, 196
  silence, importance of, 199
  summarizing reasons to buy now, 197-198
  techniques used to gain benefits, 193-203
  think *closing*, 193
  using closing questions deftly, 196
  which technique to use when, 203
Comparables in pricing property, 129-130
"Comparative Market Analysis," 97
"Comparative Market Analysis" (sample form), 96
Complaints, seller's most common, 112
Concentrating, 56-57
Contracts, 172-173
Control, key to, 138
Control of selling process *(see* Selling process, control of)
Counteroffers, 175-176, 177
"Cream puff," 89

E

Emotional motivations, 73-74
Erlicher, Harry, 34
Error, most common in selling, 34

F

Facts and figures, preparing, 28-29
Feedback, using effectively, 63-70
  benefits gained, 63-64
  checklist, 70

Feedback, using effectively *(cont'd)*
  for easier, faster, and more frequent closing, 70
  overcoming hesitation, 64-65
  techniques to gain benefits, 64-70
  turning objections into reasons to buy, 65
  using summary technique, 65-69
FHA financing, 132
Financial ability of buyer, 78-79
Financing, 132
Five P's, 31
Following through, 181-189
  benefits gained, 182
  checklist, 189
  danger of taking it for granted, 186
  giving up makes next salesperson's task easy, 182-183
  making most of each closing, 186, 188
  records for, 184-185
  remembering rewards, 189
  sales reserves, 184
  steps after sale, 185-186
  techniques to gain benefits, 182-189
  when to call, 184
  whom to call, 184
"4 Steps to Know Which Home You Can Afford," 79, 83
F's: feel, felt, and found, 220

G

Gestures, 58-59
"Go" signs, 231-232
Greif, Edwin Charles, 161
Growth and increased profit, reaching out for, 239-251
  assessing your performance, 242
  benefits gained, 240-241
  changing with changing times, 243-244
  checking pace, 243
  checklist, 250-251
  maximizing success, minimizing failure, 244-245
  overcoming slump in selling real estate, 245-246
  review of day, 241-242
  sharpening selling skills, 247
  specialization, 248-249
  techniques for gaining benefits, 241-250
  widening horizons, 248
Guidelines for storytelling, 162-163

H

Holloway, Len O., 127
"Hot buttons," 74, 156-157
*How I Multiplied My Income and
     Happiness in Selling*, 71

I

Inspection Information Form (illustration),
     94
Interest on mortgage, right to change, 114
Interruptions, handling, 140-141
Interrupting, 41
Interviews, taking charge at, 142
Information, mortgage, 114-115
Information for listing, 114
Ireland, Chris, 243

K

Keys to effective planning, 23
Key words to storytelling, 165

L

Lee, Ivy, 25
Legal description, 115
Leibowitz, Samuel S., 31
Listening, 53-62
  asking questions to demonstrate
       listening, 57-58
  benefits gained, 54-55
  checklist, 61-62
  concentrating, 56-57
  difference between hearing and listening,
       56
  effect of, 54
  with eyes, 58
  hearing and heeding buying signals,
       59-60
  meaning of, 54
  showing desire to listen, 57
  techniques used to gain benefits, 55-56
  watching for gestures, 58-59
Listing, new, 29-30
Listing presentation, planning an effective,
     89-97
  benefits gained, 91
  checklist, 97-98

Listing presentation *(cont'd)*
  handling would-be owner-sellers, 95
  inspecting property, 93
  leaving price until last, 93,95
  knowing property and homeowner, 92
  name of game, 90
  planned, not canned, 91-92
  recording specifics, 93
  techniques used to gain benefits, 91-97
Listing presentation, executing an effective,
     99-109
  benefits gained, 100-101
  checklist, 109
  insuring commission, 107
  keeping door open, 106
  Magic Listing Secret, 99-100
  perceiving problem, 101
  persuasion, 105-106
  points to ponder, 108-109
  proof of delivery or promises, 104
  return visit, 106-107
  secret, great listing, 99
  selling service, not statistics, 101
  solution, promising the, 101-104
  techniques for gaining benefits, 101-109
  using testimonial letters, 105
  understanding seller's thinking, 100
  ways to tell and show, 104-105
Loyalty, establishing, 82,84

M

Magic Listing Secret, 99-100
Magic words and phrases, using, 217-228
  for ads, 222-223
  for attracting buyer, 225
  avoiding words that repel, 226
  benefits gained, 217-218
  checklist, 227-228
  feel, felt, and found, 220
  painting a picture, 224
  to gain power over client, 227
  powerful phrases, 225-226
  short and simple, 220-221
  techniques to gain benefits, 218-227
  "when," not "if," 220
  "why," 219
  "you," 218-219
Marketing proceedings, explaining to
     seller, 119-120
Merchandising creatively, 117-118

Monthly payments on mortgage,
    variations, 114
Mortgage information, 114-115
    form for requesting, 116
    verifying, 114-115
Most effective clincher (see Storytelling)
Multiple listing, 21, 31, 82, 84
Multiple listing service, 119, 120
My Life in Court, 54

N

Negotiating table, control at, 143
Nizer, Louis, 54

O

Offers, quick acceptance of, 169-179
    arrival at house, 172
    benefits gained, 169-170
    calling for appointment, 170
    checklist, 179-180
    collaboration, 174
    controlling speech muscles, 173
    cooperating with selling agent, 177-178
    counteroffers, 175-176
    disclosing contents of contract, 172-173
    final step, 179
    handling phoning of seller, 171
    handling "we'd like to think it over,"
        176
    leaving with something specific, 177
    perils of indecision, 177
    preventing leaks, 170-171
    reporting counteroffers, 177
    sale before sale, 171-172
    seating, 172
    small difference in price, 175
    soliciting sellers' reactions, 174
    techniques to gain benefits, 170-178
    two tips, 178
    "what if," 175
    when seller says "no," 174
    word of caution, 173
Open-ended questions, 46-47
Open houses, 150-151
Overpricing (see Pricing property
    reasonably)
Overpricing, pitfalls of, 131-132

P

Planning, keys to effective, 23
Preparation, key to $750,000 sale, 30-31
Preparation for a productive day, 22-32
    benefits gained, 23-24
    checking tools, 22
    previewing houses, 22
    qualifying questionnaire, 22
    researching property, 22
    techniques to gain benefits, 24-32
Preplanning, 138
Previewing houses, 22, 149
    advantages of, 152, 153
Price adjustment, 133-134
Price reduction, 132
Pricing property reasonably, 127-135
    already half sold, 131
    benefits gained, 128-129
    checklist, 135
    comparables, 129-130
    discussing terms, 132
    peril of too high initial price, 134
    pitfalls, 131-132
    price adjustment, 133-134
    price reduction, 133
    secret of, 127
    techniques to gain benefits from
        129-135
Productive day, preparation for (see
    Preparation for a productive day)
Powerful pause technique, 40-41
Powerful words and phrases (see Magic
    words and phrases, using)
Profit, increased (see Growth and
    increased profit, reaching out for)
Property overpricing (see Pricing property
    reasonably)

Q

Qualifying the real estate buyer and seller,
    71-87
    advance agreement, 84-85
    analyzing the problem, 74-75
    benefits gained, 72
    checklist, 85-87
    emotional motivations, 73-74
    financial ability of buyer, 78-79
    handling inquiries, 75-76
    "hot buttons," 74

Qualifying the real estate buyer and seller *(cont'd)*
learning about buyer, seller, and property, 79-80
loyalty, establishing, 82, 84
myth that buyers and sellers are liars, 73
with a questionnaire, 75
quickie questionnaire, 75-76, 78
how to use, 76, 78
techniques to gain benefits, 73-85
using extra information, 80
using information from sellers, 81
walking in another's shoes, 81-82
Question, "alternate-choice," 48-49
Questionnaire, qualifying, 22, 27
Questions, open-ended, 46-47
Quick acceptance of offers (*see* Offers, quick acceptance of)

R

Request for Mortgage Information (form), 116
Researching properties, 22
Right question at the right time, 43-52
alternate choice question, 48-49
asking for the order, 49-50
benefits gained, 44-45
checklist, 51-52
for fast sale, 43-44
open-ended questions, 46-47
selling as asking, 45
techniques for gaining benefits, 45-46
using tie-downs, 47-48
"what if" questions, 49-50
Roth, Charles B., 161, 237

S

"Sales reserves," 184
Schwab, Charles, 25
Secrets of Closing Sales, 237
Seller's role, 120-121
Selling as asking, 45
Selling process, control of, 137-146
avoiding "we'll call you" syndrome 141-142
benefits gained, 138
checklist, 145-146
control at negotiating table, 143
planning ahead, 138

Selling process, control of *(cont'd)*
resisting intimidation, 143-145
setting stage, 139
taking charge at listing interviews, 142
techniques to gain benefits, 138-146
tested tips, 139-141
"change the subject" technique, 141
handling interruption, 140
sidetracking, 139-140
Selling situations, eight real estate, 24-25
Servicing the listing effectively, 111-125
advertising media, 117
after sale, 123
avoidance of seller's most common complaint, 112-113
benefits gained, 113-114
checking legal description, 115
checklist, 124-125
extra service, 123
extending listing before expiration, 122-123
helpful hints, 118
inclusions and exclusions, 117
marketing procedures explained, 119-120
merchandising creatively, 117-118
reporting regularly, 122
response from ads, 119
rules for writing ads, 118
seller's role, 120-121
techniques to gain benefits, 114-125
telephone information, 115
verifying mortgage information, 114-115
Showing property effectively, 147-158
appointments, 153
arrival at house, 154-155
benefits gained, 148
best route, 153-154
checklist, 158-159
do's and don'ts, 151-152
formula for, 148-149
joy of discovery, 155
key review points, 151-153
last step, 150
making most of showing, 155-157
focusing on "hot buttons," 155-157
heeding buying signals, 157
lingering, 155
listening to reactions, 157
second look, 156
soliciting opinions, 155-156
meeting prospects, 154
number of houses, 153

Showing property effectively *(cont'd)*
  open houses, 150-151
  previewing, 149
  selecting right houses, 149
  sequence, 153
  techniques to gain benefits, 148-158
  tip-off clue, 157-158
Sidetracking, avoidance of, 139-140
Stone, David, 222
Storytelling, 161-167
  at any time, 163-164
  benefits gained, 162
  checklist, 166-167
  guidelines, 162-163
    correctness, 163
    fitness to buyers and sellers, 163
    make interesting, 163
    to the point, 163
  key words, 165
  last resort, 164-165
  techniques to gain benefits, 162-166
  use of witnesses, 165-166
  various ways to use, 166
Summary technique, 65-69

T

Talking too much, 33-42
  arguing, 41-42
  benefits gained by silence, 36
  interrupting, 41
  introducing objections, 37-38
  not paying attention, 42
  powerful pause technique, 40-41
  refraining from, 33-34
  repeating certain words, 42
  saving the ammunition, 38-39
  telephone calls, 36-37
Telephone, taking maximum advantage of,
    205-215
  for appointments, not sales, 208
  benefits gained, 205-206

Telephone, taking maximum advantage of
    (cont'd)
  calls to attorneys, 211-212
  checklist, 214-215
  controlling conversation to direction of
    call, 207-208
  disciplined use of, 206-207
  improving telephone personality,
    213-214
  inquiry about advertisement, 208-210
  making calls pay off, 214
  reply to request for address, 210-211
  settling problems between buyer and
    seller, 212-213
  smile in voice, 207
  techniques to gain benefits, 206-214
Telephone, receiving information over, 115
Testimonial letters, 105
"Things to Do Today," 25, 27
"Things to Do Today" (sample form), 26
Tie-downs, 47-48
Training Manual for Real Estate Salesmen,
    222
*The 22 Biggest Mistakes Managers Make
    and How to Correct Them*, 243

V

VA financing, 132
Van Fleet, James K., 243

W

"We'll call you" syndrome, 141-142
"What if" question, 49-50
"Why," use of, 219
"When," use of, 220
Witnesses, used in selling, 165-166

Y

"You," use of, 218-219